PICK NICK

PICK NICK

The Political Odyssey of
Nick Galifianakis
from Immigrant Son
to Congressman

JOHN E. SEMONCHE

tidal
PRESS

TABLE OF CONTENTS

OVERTURE

The Galifianakis Name:
Liability or Asset in the Land of Dixie?

Whether any other surname has ever played a more prominent role in a political career is doubtful. The musical mouthful proclaimed Nick's Greek roots so clearly that Kay Kyser, the bandleader and radio personality, quipped: "I don't know whether you are supposed to spell it or sneeze it." Yet, it certainly stood out, and eventually Nick was able to use it to his advantage. When asked how to spell it, he would say: "It begins with a Gal and ends with a Kiss," instantly revealing his good nature. Declaring his name was too long to fit on a single button, he frequently employed two. People may have had trouble pronouncing the name, but they loved the buttons.

His mother liked to tell a story about her eldest son and the family name. One day when Nick was nine years old and enrolled at the Fuller School in Durham, he came home saying that he was being teased because of his name, a name that even the teachers could not pronounce or remember. Mama Sophie wisely responded that he should pray to God for a name that everyone would remember.

Galifianakis' Northern political colleagues and many observers puzzled over how a person with such a long and clearly ethnic name could be elected in a Southern state where names usually had at most two syllables. (Galifianakis pronounced phonetically would have six syllables, Gal i fi an ak is, but as far back as Nick could remember, it was always pronounced ignoring the second i, Gal i fan ak is, thus reducing the challenge it posed to five syllables.) After all, "outsiders" and "agitators", sometimes with long and unfamiliar names, were being blamed for disrupting the South's status quo. Nick would fight the characterization, asking how could he be an outsider when he was born and raised in North Carolina? Although change was beginning in the 1960s, some public personalities, including entertainers, still shortened or changed their foreign-sounding names.

Five decades later, with continued migration from the North and Middle West, the South has become far more heterogeneous and people are now far more proficient in dealing with foreign sounding names. For instance, no one seems to have trouble pronouncing the name of the Duke University basketball coach, Mike Krzyzewski, or, for that matter, Nick's nephew, Zach Galifianakis, the comedian and actor.

CHAPTER I

From Crete to "God Bless America"
in Durham, North Carolina

Nick's father, Emmanuel Galifianakis, was born in 1890 on the island of Crete, one of the many islands in the Mediterranean Sea belonging to Greece. He arrived in the United States in just before the First World War halted the Great Migration from Southern and Eastern Europe. Emmanuel was one of 450,000 Greeks who came to America between 1890 and 1917. The immigrants were largely bachelors; males constituted 90% of the Greek immigrants as compared, for instance, to Italians, who were less than 60% male. They faced steep hurdles to acceptance in their new country. To the consternation of many earlier immigrants who came from northern Europe, the United States was being transformed at the turn of the twentieth century in a way not to their liking. A forty-two volume Senate report in 1907 blamed the country's troubles with crime on these new immigrants from southern and eastern Europe, who were deemed to be "resistant" to the melting pot that had absorbed peoples from northern Europe. In fact, when general immigration restriction on Europeans first came in the 1920s, quotas were allocated not on the basis of the ethnic mix of the population at that time but rather on the basis of the composition of that population in 1890, well before the change in who was immigrating had occurred. The country has always struggled with a tribal desire to close the door.

Emmanuel knew that he did not want to till the arid land as his ancestors had in the small village of Sgourokefali. He had no formal education but he could converse in a number of languages and often quoted Socrates. As an adolescent he left Crete for Egypt, heading first to Cairo and then on to Alexandria where he found work in a pasta factory, which he inherited on the owner's death. He sold that factory and with part of the proceeds purchased a ticket to the United States. Emmanuel sailed for America in 1913.

Nick's father, Emmanuel Galifianakis, and Emmanuel's cousin, E.D. Catala.

Like so many of the new immigrants of that era, he was processed through Ellis Island and initially settled in New York City. His first concession to being Americanized was to begin answering to the name Mike. He scrubbed rest rooms in the Roosevelt Hotel and soon moved to Cleveland, where a substantial Greek community existed. Work brought him south to a munitions plant in Hopewell, Virginia that the E.I. Du Pont de Nemours Company had recently built. The outbreak of war in Europe in August 1914 and the need for the United States to envision the possibility of participation in that war led to the expansion of the workforce and production at the Virginia facility. Good pay attracted Mike and others to the town near Richmond at the confluence of the James and Appomattox rivers.

As the demand for munitions lessened near the end of World War I, Du Pont cut back its production and workforce. Perhaps the weather in the area had been more to his liking than that of Cleveland, for instead of returning to Cleveland Mike moved further south to Durham, North Carolina. He was the first Greek to come to the community from the island of Crete, and it would be three years before another Cretan, Emmanuel Catala arrived in 1922. As with so many of his fellow Greek immigrants, Mike found work supplying food to hungry residents.

The town that Mike encountered was growing and changing. Durham had less than a hundred inhabitants at the end of the Civil War and was only incorporated in 1869. Spurred on by industrial growth, as were so many areas during the great industrial push of the latter third of the nineteenth century, the city reached a population of 6,679 by 1900 and then tripled in size to 21,719 by 1920. By 1940 it would triple again to 60,195. For better or worse, Durham was ahead of its time, prohibiting the sale of alcoholic beverages and closing its saloons in 1903, well before the nation as a whole began its great experiment with prohibition. The state of North Carolina followed suit in 1908. Durham also had the state's first free public library, which was established in 1898.

By 1900, the tobacco and textile industries had put Durham on the map as one of the state's richest cities and a place where one might go to find one's fortune. No millionaires came to Durham but the town made millionaires out of some of the enterprising young men who saw its promise, including J. S. Carr of the Blackwell Durham Tobacco Company, reputedly the state's first millionaire. Eventually, of course, Washington Duke and his sons were able to consolidate cigarette manufacturing and form the American Tobacco Company in 1890. Durham was the center of the North Carolina's tobacco industry. The city was also a textile manufacturing hub, home to one of the state's largest employers, Erwin Mills, which built its first manufacturing plant in the town in 1893. Durham also had the largest fertilizer plant in the state. There was, in short, great economic opportunity, and it became available to a more inclusive group than many other places in the South.

In the post-Reconstruction South, which was becoming even more white-controlled after the widespread disenfranchisement of blacks in the 1890s, Durham was different. Despite white-control, there were real opportunities available for blacks to become successful. In 1920, blacks constituted about 35% of the population, a proportion that was only a few percentage points higher thirty years later. They had come to the town in increasing numbers and worked in all capacities, just as whites did. The growth of insurance and banking establishments serving blacks helped create a black middle class that was quite unusual in both the state and in the South. The black-owned North Carolina Mutual Life Insurance Company was established in 1898 and thrives today. Furthermore, many of these middle-class blacks accepted the obligation to serve the community in various ways.

Durham, therefore, was celebrated for the opportunities it provided not only to whites but to blacks as well. In fact, both Booker T. Washington and William E. B. Du Bois, who seldom agreed, sang the praises of the town in harmony. Washington, in 1903, characterized Durham as "the city of Cities to look for prosperity of the Negroes and the greatest amount of friendly feeling between the two races of the South." Almost a decade later, Du Bois praised the accomplishments of Durham blacks, finding their "social and economic development . . . more striking than that of any similar group in the nation."

Public education began slowly in the 1880s, with public school and private schools levying about the same fees. The beginnings of higher education in Durham trace back to 1882 when Trinity College, which eventually became Duke University, moved from near High Point to Durham. Durham had outmaneuvered Raleigh for the school by providing attractive incentives. The tobacco magnates J. S. Carr and Washington Duke donated a large tract of land and contributed $85,000, respectively. Not until 1905 did Durham have a high school, though. Before a citywide educational system was created, black leaders had established schools. For blacks seeking higher education, North Carolina College, which eventually became a part of the University of North Carolina system, was founded in 1910 as the National Religious Training School and Chautauqua. Its purpose was to train black ministers but within six years the school's leaders expanded that original purpose to include accepting all blacks who sought higher education. The state purchased the private school and assumed control in 1923, well before the United States Supreme Court would order all states to provide equal higher education for all its citizens.

In stark contrast to the substantial percentage of blacks in Durham, only twenty foreign-born individuals lived in the town in 1900, making it a community with one of the lowest percentages of foreign-born in a nation where 14% of the population had been born in other countries. Clearly most new immigrants skirted the South, finding other parts of the country more comfortable and welcoming. That would start to change slowly before Emmanuel—now Mike—Galifianakis arrived. By 1910, the number of foreign-born citizens had risen to 258 and would continue to climb.

Immigrants usually clustered together in the United States, not only in big cities but in smaller ones as well. One family member tended to bring other family members, then acquaintances, and over time an ethnic enclave was established. The arrival of Greeks in Durham dates back to 1901 when three teenagers moved to the town. In the next year, George and Andrew S. Trakas, along with Nick D. Karres, established a business, Trakas and Company Confectionary, that catered to the sweet-tooths in town. Within three years, the proprietors welcomed Matthew and Frank Karres, brothers of Nick Karres, and Gus Pappas and Theo Lambris. By then, the company had established quite a reputation as purveyors of candies and ice cream and had expanded into Virginia and South Carolina. The Durham store changed hands, each time being sold to immigrant Greeks, and eventually became the Marathon Candy Kitchen. What made the shops even more attractive was their stocking of fresh fruit, which was only available at these sweet shops.

In addition to the confectionery business, Greeks opened cafes in Durham. They often changed hands but still usually within the growing Greek community. There was the Metropolitan Café, the Busy Bee Café, the New York Café and Restaurant, the People's Lunch, the Royal Café, the Durham Café, and the Phoenix Café. Mike Galifianakis got into the business shortly after his arrival in 1919 by opening Mike's Weenie Stand. Soon he would have two hot dog stands.

The proprietors of these businesses were almost exclusively single men. The first local marriage occurred in 1914, when Manuel Capsalis married Fotini Pavlakis after her arrival from New York. Their son, Otis, was the first person born in Durham to be baptized in the Greek Orthodox ritual. Other families eventually joined the Pavlakises, and the first marriage among the Durham group took place in 1922 when Charles Dackis and Pachalia Boulakis were wed. Any Greek Orthodox ceremony at that time had to be performed by a priest who travelled from Richmond, Virginia. Otherwise, people seeking to wed had to make the trip north themselves. In 1925, a Greek Orthodox Church, Holy Trinity, was established in Raleigh, twenty-five miles east of Durham. Arrangements were made for monthly services in Durham in the parish house of Saint Philip's Episcopal Church. Despite the increase in numbers of Greek immigrants and their closeness, it took until 1945 for a Greek Orthodox Church to be formed in Durham. When that finally happened, Mike Galifianakis was elected to serve on the parish council.

Mike had found a place to call home, and he had done well enough with the hot dog stands to open a restaurant in 1920. His establishment supplanted Page's Café at the same address, and he named his restaurant the Lincoln Café. None of the cafés owned by Greeks had names that reflected their owners' ethnic background. For Mike, naming the new café after Abraham Lincoln was an act of patriotism. If the name rankled white Southerners, so be it. Although Durham in the 1920s, as it had been for years, was a good place for single men to succeed, Mike, now in his mid-30s, yearned for family life. His busy commercial life left little time for getting acquainted with the opposite sex, leading him to think increasingly about going back to Crete to find a bride.

However, first he had to anchor himself in his new land by becoming an American citizen. He took the oath in 1926, as he proudly renounced old loyalties and embraced his new country. To Mike, the United States of America was a country filled with promise. While some immigrants yearned to return to the Old World, he found the New World so much more attractive. He loved his new country and not only proudly displayed its flag, but took any criticism of the United States as a personal insult. As was often the case, he, as a foreign-born naturalized citizen, was more intimately attached to his adopted country than many native-born citizens. He believed in both God and America, so when he said, as he often did, "God Bless America," he said it with a prayerful conviction. Just as he would hear nothing negative about his new country, he would feel the same way about his fellow human beings. A believer in the old adage that if you have nothing good to say about another person, then say nothing at all, Mike took it a step further by finding something good in everyone.

After becoming an American citizen, Mike sailed for Crete to seek a bride. He found a young woman he had known as a child named Sophia Kastrinakis, an eighteen-year old who he assured would easily find a home in the growing Greek community in Durham. He waived the Old World requirement of a dowry and married the young woman, just half his age. She did not return to Durham with her new husband, who felt that he wanted her to come only when he had a house she could call home. Several months later, accompanied by one of Mike's cousins, George Chronaki, she arrived in Durham. For his efforts, Chronaki was given a 50% interest in the Lincoln Café, and he and Mike would work as equal partners for the next thirty years.

Nick's parents, Emmanuel, now Mike, with his wife, Sophia, preganant with Nick.

Sophia must have been apprehensive about her journey from a rural home in Crete to the bustling town of Durham. However, the house Mike had bought for them at 308 South Markham Street was in the middle of a Greek community. Two other houses on Markham were owned by fellow Greeks as were two others around the corner on Roxboro Road. The young bride, therefore, was able to adjust quickly to her new life. She soon developed an easy and welcoming manner that made her quite recognizable as a leading Durham citizen, known to all as Mama or Miss Sophie, the wife of Mr. Mike. Mike joked that that Sophia's first English words were "charge it to Mr. Mike." Sophia was comfortable with others, like her husband, no matter what their social and economic status. Her home was always open and she would eagerly share her food with both friends and strangers. Mike and Sophia would have five children, all boys. Nick was the first, followed by Mike Jr., Harry, Peter, and John.

Maybe as a way of connecting with their roots, Mike and Sophia would never lose their Greek accents, even as their English improved.

INTERLUDE 1

Nick's Father and the Lincoln Café

The Lincoln Café was located at 114 South Magnum Street. The café opened at 5 a.m. to provide breakfast to workers completing their night shifts. In the café's window each morning eggs were arranged in a pyramid, and by the 6 a.m. the pyramid was gone. Although Mike at times would prepare Greek dishes for fellow Greeks, the restaurant served American soul and comfort food. The embrace of ethnic food in the country would only come later and to survive, the Lincoln Café had to serve what people wanted to eat. It quickly became a welcoming gathering place that brought people of all classes and races together. Mike Galifianakis believed that each customer deserved the same service and respect, so even though initially a partition separated the dining areas for blacks and whites, as was customary at the time, that partition was gone long before meaningful integration began to take place in the rest of Durham. The counter, originally designated for whites, was integrated first. On the weekends well-dressed blacks and whites would come to listen to the jukebox or, at rare times, a live performance by Fats Domino or Nat King Cole, when they were in town for other engagements.

During the extended depression of the 1930s when money was tight, Mr. Mike accepted IOUs from both black and white patrons, including many prominent citizens who subsequently became quite financially comfortable. When Mike died in 1958, a batch of these IOUs was found among his papers, some scribbled on napkins. The statute of limitations on collecting these debts had long passed, and apparently they had been forgotten by some of the people who had benefitted from Mike's generosity. Mike was by nature more worried about paying his share than collecting money owed to him. In fact, Mike's patriotism was so strong that he worried, during his yearly filing of taxes, whether Uncle Sam was receiving all that was due.

All of Mike's sons at one time or another worked in various capacities in the restaurant, but as adults, their education and talents would take them elsewhere.

CHAPTER II

The Early Years, 1928-1947

Mike was absolutely delighted when on July 22, 1928, Sophia presented him with Nicholas, the first of their five sons. They would all be born in the United States, except for Peter, who was born on the family visit to Crete in 1938. In Greek culture, as in many others, boy children were especially revered, and the first-born even more so. Sophia would not disagree, and she never missed an opportunity to tell the story about the family's first visit to Washington, D. C. taken when Nick was only a month old. They were in Washington to see family, but she and Mike slipped away one afternoon to go to the Capitol. She told her husband she wanted to do this alone, but he stayed near. Carrying Nick, slowly she mounted the Capitol steps finally reaching the rotunda inside. Sophie placed her baby boy under the dome, and knelt down beside him. She paid no attention to a group of tourists who stopped to witness the strange proceedings. Placing her hands together she looked upward and in a strong and clear voice spoke in Greek and then, for good measure, repeated what she had said. "What language is she speaking?" a person in the crowd asked. Hearing the question, Mike in his accented English answered: "Greek." Someone else asked, "What's that she's saying?" Mike didn't seem to mind the questions or the crowd; in fact, he seemed pleased to share this private family moment with them. He responded: "She's praying that our son will grow up to become a great man and do much good." When the small crowd applauded, Sophie, somewhat self-consciously, picked Nick up and came over to her husband. She whispered to him. Answering the quizzical expressions of the interested onlookers, he translated: "She heard God say 'Yes.'"

Whether this episode ever actually occurred is doubtful, but it was obvious that when Sophie told the story, she believed every word of it. The Cretan village girl talked of her premonitions throughout her life; such things were part of the rural life in which she was raised. Living in this new country would not change her. Both parents agreed that their son would not succeed his father in the food business because he was destined for greater things, perhaps even the presidency itself.

The values Nick Galifianakis would cherish for a lifetime were those that his parents had taught him early, largely by example. His father was a generous soul, who would feed the hungry during the depression of the 1930s, and always asserted that one's highest duty was to love and serve one's country. His father's love of his adopted country imposed upon Nick a special responsibility to discharge those obligations his father felt toward his country. The son completely absorbed his father's patriotism, not in his father's uncritical sense, but in the sense that the country had a destiny to fulfill so that it could remain an enviable model for others.

Even more than the honesty and patriotism that he exemplified, his father stressed moderation "in all thy ways." From his mother, Nick would take her love of people, her willingness to help others, and her ready acceptance of people no matter how different they were. Nick's parents also worked to instill confidence in Nick that he could do anything. That belief would result in a self-assurance that established the young man's base for achievement. His self-confidence never became overbearing; in fact, he often expressed surprise when others valued what he had done. Nick not only found something to admire and respect in everyone he met, but he inspired others with his belief in them. As would often be recognized, he was likeable, an important personal asset for an individual whose greatest desire was to serve. An "aw shucks" attitude made him one of the "old boys," and it tended to bring out the mothering instinct in women. Nick's values would be tested, but generally he met the challenges. Mike would not survive to see his eldest son in politics, but Nick always felt that his father would have been proud. As the eldest son, much was expected of Nick. In age, he was closest to Mike, the second son, but even Mike deferred to the "captain," as Nick was called. The title would impose new responsibilities on Nick, especially after his father died in 1958, responsibilities that would continue into the indefinite future.

For a person who made his way in the world without any formal education, Mike was a devout believer in the worth of formal education, something he insisted that all his sons have. Greek was spoken at home with the hope that the boys would be bilingual. In fact, many of the Durham Greek families hired a teacher who provided formal instruction in their native language.

Nick did well in school and seemed more mature than his classmates, which led to early positions of responsibility, some assigned and some assumed. At Fuller Elementary School, he was made a member of the safety patrol. In that capacity, he and another student were responsible for saving the life of a younger student who had wandered in the path of an oncoming automobile. Both boys hurled their bodies at the errant student, knocking her out of the way of the car. Jack Holt, a fellow member of the school safety patrol, was credited with the heroic act. As part of the honor conferred upon him he was asked to assume the role of leader of a parade in Washington, D.C. His only spoken task was to bellow out "Eyes Right" as the parade passed in front of President Franklin D. Roosevelt. Basically shy, Holt eagerly accepted Nick's offer to do the job for him.

Fuller School, reputed to be the best elementary school in Durham, was very close to the Galifianakis home, across from the First Baptist Church. Although gregarious, Nick was not especially ambitious at this young age. When his first grade teacher, Mrs. Allbright, asked students what they wanted to be when they grew up, Nick consistently said that he wanted to be a street sweeper. It may not have helped that with Greek spoken at home, Nick was not completely comfortable speaking English until the second grade. However, his teachers realized that Nick was not only a fine student with a keen sense of responsibility, but also that he had some artistic talent. A class project involved the making of papier-mâché animals. The teacher was so impressed with Nick's work that she had the animals that he had created displayed in the school cafeteria. In fact, when the Fuller School burned to the ground during Nick's time there, no lives were lost, but among the losses specifically lamented by many were Nick's animals.

In 1938, when Nick was ten, and his brothers Mike and Harry were eight and six, the family, minus the patriarch who had to tend to his business in Durham, sailed for Greece. Nick's parents wanted the children to get to know their extended family on Crete. Nick's father never knew his own father, John, but his mother was still alive, as were Sophie's parents. Nick remembers learning much about both grapes and olives, along with a little ancient Greek history. They stayed for a year, and the family grew by one when Peter was born on the island. Unfortunately, Mike's arrival to bring the family home at the end of their stay came six days after his mother died, but he was pleased that his sons had been able to spend time with her.

The boys had much to tell their friends on their return to Durham, including how on the trip home on the eve of World War II, Nick ran into trouble when the ship stopped in Italy. The 11-year-old was arrested for counting the submarines in the port. After his father, who spoke Italian enough to berate the authorities for arresting a boy who could hardly be a spy, intervened, Nick was released.

Since the Fuller School had burned down in his absence, Nick completed grammar school in North Durham then attended Central Junior High School (later Carr Middle School). He was a natural athlete and excelled in many sports. He was a member of Central Junior High's baseball team which also included Roger Craig, who would go on to become a major league pitcher and manager. Upon graduation from Central, Nick was awarded medals for being the "best school citizen" in the 9th grade and for his work with the Student Council and the Literary Club.

Football was the premier sport at Durham High School, and Nick had both the size and talent to participate. However, when Nick was knocked out in a football scrimmage and carried home to his mother, she made him promise never to play the game again. (In Greece, her younger brother, playing soccer, had gotten kicked in the head and died from the injury. Sophie told Nick she had a premonition that her brother would be injured playing that game.) Nick reluctantly agreed, serving instead as manager for the Durham High team. And true to his word he passed on an offer of a football scholarship to Duke University. He was successful, however, in convincing his mother that his brothers should be allowed to play football, given that she had no premonitions about them. Harry would eventually play varsity football at North Carolina State University and Mike would play with Charlie "Choo Choo" Justice at the University of North Carolina in Chapel Hill.

Unable to play football, Nick was confined to track and field. He was part of a Durham High relay team that won the Eastern Class AA Conference title and then successfully defended its state title in a meet in Chapel Hill the following week. The team also participated in the Penn Relays in Philadelphia and the C Club track meet in Washington.

In addition to sports, Nick was involved in a wide variety of extra-curricular activities in high school, often taking on leadership roles. Although he came in second in a county-wide American Legion oratorical contest in March of 1947 (after earlier winning the school contest speaking on "The Constitution—Temple of Liberty"), he was generally chosen to be the speaker whenever a need for one arose. Nick's high school Latin teacher said he could sway student opinion with his skills and concluded: "If you wanted anything done, the whole school turned to Nick." Whether seeking contributions for the Student Council's budget or the Community Fund, Nick would urge students to carry their share of the burden. Acknowledging Nick's skills with a premonition of her own, Nick's ninth grade civics teacher, Mrs. Heflin, remarked that he had all the makings of a politician.

Yet Nick had more than people skills. He regularly made the honor roll and enjoyed remarkable academic success. The November 22, 1946 lead story in the *Hi-Rocket*, the award-winning student newspaper, was "Galifianakis Wins

Nick's yearbook. Note how his is the largest paragraph of activities.

'Prof. Quiz' Contest Held in Auditorium." The first part of the first sentence summed up the student body's well known opinion of their classmate: "Well-know and well-liked Nick Galifianakis...." The story then went on to chronicle Nick's success in a knowledge quiz sponsored by the American Oil Company. The quizzes were administered by Craig Earl, known as Professor Quiz, at high schools around the country. In the Durham High version fourteen students were initially chosen to compete, the number being reduced to five after the first round. This test of general knowledge gave the students ten seconds to respond; an incorrect response or no answer led to the student's removal from the group. The highest possible score a person could get was 600, and Nick emerged the victor with a score of 475. Surprised at the outcome, Nick was assured by Professor Quiz that the score was better than that accumulated by Yale University students when the same questions were asked.

Among his many varied activities, Nick wrote a column titled "Nickelodian," a humor column with puns and poems, for the *Hi-Rocket*, There was no activity that didn't attract Nick, as he played a part in *The Barretts of Wimpole Street*, the senior play, and helped wash and paint the Student Council room.

When a classmate, Jimmy Rutherford, was asked to write a paper on "the most unforgettable character I ever met," he chose Nick. Jimmy said Nick was always happy, optimistic, friendly and kind. Jimmy wrote that the only criticism the teachers had of Nick was his boisterous energy and not ever "being serious." Then Jimmy hit on another trait that would characterize Galifianakis throughout his life when he quoted his subject as saying "I would like to walk in a big silly formal affair with old clothes on and slap the old snoots on their backs and liven up the place." This tendency to eschew formality and stuffiness by playing the oaf was an essential part of Nick's well recognized sense of humor.

On June 2, 1947 Nick graduated with 266 other seniors. However he was the only one singled out for a special tribute in the *Hi-Rocket*, headlined: "Nick G. Leaves Mark on Durham High." The article began "His ever-abundant humor and capable efficiency have marked Nick Galifianakis as a memorable figure of the class of '47." It mentioned his many activities, including his winning the interscholastic shot put competition. The article concluded as follows:

Nick upon his high school graduation.

"In the furthering of a well-founded school career we wish Nick Galifianakis the best of luck. He has left an everlasting mark upon Durham High, and we will remember him with pride and appreciation." In a final awards ceremony at the school, Nick was also the star. He received the Citizenship Award and with it a loving cup. The cup became the receptacle for the physical embodiments of his other awards. As each award was announced Nick dropped it in the loving cup causing a sound that echoed throughout the auditorium. As the awards to Nick mounted up the audience began to snicker, though not Nick's parents. The tears that escaped his father's eyes testified to the pride he felt as others recognized the achievements of his eldest son.

Nick enjoyed his high school years and would remain that same person who graduated from Durham High for the rest of his life. For Nick the future was bright and seemed to promise that the best was yet to come.

INTERLUDE 2

Success at North Carolina Boys State, 1946

Between his junior and senior year at Durham High, Nick was selected to attend North Carolina's Boys State. Founded in Illinois in 1935 by Hayes Kennedy and Harold Card, the Boys State program was designed to immerse students in the mechanics of representative government. The students would elect officials who would then participate in simulated local, county and state government activities during one week in the summer. The idea took hold, and by 1946 every one of the forty-eight states, under the auspices of the American Legion, had such programs.

In North Carolina the program was conducted by Albert Coates and the institution he created and headed, the Institute of Government at the University in Chapel Hill. Nick with five of his fellow Durham High students attended Boys State from September 1-8, 1946. The annual recreation of a political community composed of youngsters had been suspended during World War II, so the 1946 gathering was the first held since 1941. One hundred and thirteen student delegates heard from a diverse group of speakers ranging from Kay Kyser, the band leader, to Carl Snavely, the University of North Carolina football coach. The talks were about citizenship and government and its functions. Coates was joined in 1946 by the assistant director of the Institute of Government, Terry Sanford, who would become the state's governor and U. S. Senator. Nick gained the attention not only of Sanford but also of William C. (Bill) Friday, who would become president of the University of North Carolina system.

Those counselors urged Nick to run for governor of Boys State. Nick so eagerly embraced the experience of the simulated political environment and made friends so easily that the counselors saw only victory ahead. Nick later said he felt that Sanford and Friday were in part motivated by the challenge of seeing whether, with their help, a boy with the name of Galifianakis could really win the election. Nick did win and Friday recalled that he and Sanford did little, attributing Nick's victory to his personality and outgoing nature. Durham High School did extremely well at Boys State 1946. Durham High's student body president, Buck Roberts, was elected lieutenant governor and won the oratorical contest at the gathering.

Boys State at UNC. Nick is in the middle of the second row.

One of Nick's responsibilities as governor was to address the Boys State General Assembly and recommend matters that it should address with legislation. Among other subjects he stressed two. Noting that the state ranked near the top in the number of potential war draftees rejected on the basis of health issues, he pronounced North Carolinians an "unhealthy people." This was the result, he said, of the lack of doctors, hospitals, clinics, and health education generally. The other issue he highlighted was one the state is still wrestling with today—financing public education. Nick stressed the need to provide adequate compensation for teachers "to insure that we keep qualified teachers...to replace those who are temporarily employed but who are unqualified, and to attract more of our young people to choose teaching as a profession."

John E. Semonche

CHAPTER III

The Years of Preparation, 1947-1960

The Duke University Nick entered in the fall of 1947 was, as were so many college campuses of the time, bustling with activity. During the war, the university was home to one of the largest V-12 military training programs created by the U.S. Navy in conjunction with over 130 colleges across the country. Although the program ended with the war, Duke was now bulging at the seams with returning veterans. Trinity College, the men's undergraduate component of the University, enrolled 2,527 first-year students in 1946, the majority of whom were returning veterans. That was the result of an admissions policy that put recent high school graduates third on a priority list that gave first preference to returning veterans who were Duke students at the time they left for military service and second preference to other veterans. Even the Women's College, whose admissions policies were highly selective, saw a peak total enrollment that year of 5,121. Furthermore, the campus was filled with construction equipment, for when building materials were released for civilian use the school began an extensive building campaign.

The Gothic buildings that give Duke its distinctive architectural character were built from 1927 to 1932, when the iconic chapel was completed. These buildings housed Trinity College, the men's-only preserve, and the professional schools. Although the institution could trace its antecedents back to 1838, its rise to prominence and its history as a research university began in 1924 when it took on its present name and became the chief beneficiary of the Duke Endowment. Tuition at the private school with Methodist ties from 1930 through 1945 had been $200 a year. In 1946 it was raised to $300, and in 1947, Nick's entering year, to $350. Post-war faculty salaries had not kept up with inflation, and much of the increase was devoted to keeping and obtaining faculty by raising their salaries.

Nick in 1949 on the 100th anniversary of the city of Durham.

Nick at nineteen was considerably younger than many of his classmates, but in 1947 the students at Duke were considerably different from those who had preceded them. In his first year, Nick took advantage of a $500 schol-arship he had received and lived on campus. He did very well academically. From 1932 to 2005, Duke University had a chapter of Phi Eta Sigma, a freshmen honor society that required a GPA of at least 3.5 for admittance. Nick became a member based upon his impressive freshman record. For his five subsequent years at Duke he would live at home, less than three miles away. As a student who lived at home, he was less of an anomaly in these immediate post-war years than he would have been both before the war and well after the war. Returning veterans, many of whom had wives and children, were creating a new normal in which "townies" were not marginalized as before.

The young man from Durham with the long ethnic name ploughed ahead with the same confidence and engaging manner that had won him that special tribute in the *Hi-Rocket*. That manner earned him election as president of the freshman class, a victory that Nick attributed to his platform: "A soap dish in every shower in the residence halls and a pencil sharpener in every classroom." School officials reprimanded him for not consulting them prior to such promises, but the result was what the young politician promised: soap dishes and pencil sharpeners in the appropriate places. Even without the attractive platform in the following year, Galifianakis was elected president of what was now the sophomore class. Apparently even returning veterans found this campus politician attractive. Yet Nick would always deny that he initiated these campaigns, instead seeing himself as a drafted candidate for these offices.

However, whether he initiated such contests or not, he was an eager competitor. And he enjoyed both highbrow and lowbrow contests. As an example of the latter, he and the vice-president of the freshman class decided to see who could date more Women's College students. A date would consist of any activity pairing the young man with a young woman that was the result of the woman saying yes to the man's request. A date had no time limit, and could range from saying yes to an invitation to have a soda together to something involving a more substantial time commitment. Both young men had well over a dozen dates, as Nick remembers the episode, but he lost when time expired and the vice-president was ahead by one date. This dating frivolity suited Nick quite well, for he had no interest in a more serious relationship. He had a career to build.

Two victories as president of his class led Nick to become a candidate for student body president in his third year at Duke. He ran as the Student Party candidate. His main competitor was an athlete named Jim Young, who was the Union Party's choice. As the votes were counted, Galifianakis and Young played bridge, until their partners gave out. The vote counting went on long into the night. When Young was finally declared the winner by nine votes, cries of fraud were heard as far away as New York City, where *Life* magazine took an interest. A Duke official told Nick not to talk to the reporter from *Life*, and he did not. Nick, by nature and upbringing, was at times quite willing to defer to the judgement of others. But his supporters pushed on and found enough fraudulent votes to determine that Nick had actually won the election by eighteen votes. The fraud was perpetrated because freshman engineering students were included as eligible voters on two lists, meaning that any unscrupulous student could vote twice, as long as his vote was cast at two different polling places. Since Young carried the engineering students by a wide margin, it was clear that he had reaped the benefit of the eager supporters who took advantage by voting twice.

The student newspaper, the *Duke Chronicle,* said only a new election for student body president would make things right. In the meantime, Young had asked Galifianakis not to contest the result. Seeing how very much Jim desired the office, Nick complied. Many years later their paths would cross again, this time in Washington, D. C. Young told Nick that the election had long troubled his conscience and that, even at this late date, he would appreciate Nick accepting an apology. Galifianakis, of course, did.

Whether this episode had an impact or not, Nick decided that he would forego his senior year and enter Duke University's School of Law. As was the case with a number of law schools, Duke had a program in which able students could seek admission after three years in the undergraduate school and, if accepted, receive their A.B. degree after completing the first year of law school. The law school was on the verge of entering the top tier of the nation's law schools, and Nick eagerly began his law study, confident that this type of graduate education was the best launching pad for his future.

The Duke law school was relatively small as law schools go and would not graduate its first class of over 100 until 1967. As such, the relationship between professor and student was closer than it would later become, and Nick took advantage of this arrangement and would be well remembered by the faculty years later. During his three years, he served as an associate editor of the law school newspaper, as a member of the editorial board of the *Duke Law Journal*, and as vice-president of the Duke Bar Association. Although the average graduating class size in the 1950s was 52, Nick's class suffered from substantial attrition. His graduating class numbered just 24, a little over a third of the students who began the course of study with him. After completion of the first year at the law school in 1951, Nick received his A.B. degree.

Law school graduation with classmate Alexander Byron

For the first time in his academic career, though, Nick was not at the top of his class. Yet no faculty member would have predicted any less than a stellar career for Nick. And indeed over the years, whenever a law school professor was asked to suggest a lawyer either for legal work or simply to introduce a new member to the bar, the name that most readily came to mind was Nick Galifianakis.

Having been deferred during his six years at Duke,

Nick realized that at some point he would be called upon to serve in the military. With his education behind him and a legal career that could wait, he considered enlisting in the U. S. Navy. How he ended up joining the U. S. Marines could be called an accident. He had gone to Boston in 1953 to accompany a friend to take a test for Officer Candidate School (OCS). Nick's friend failed the test leading the female recruiting officer to cast aspersions on the intelligence of Southerners. Nick told her that his friend was a Northerner and that he was the Southerner. She challenged him to take the test to prove her wrong. Nick could not resist the challenge. When he scored impressively on the test and then passed the physical after a tooth was extracted, the recruiter's interest skyrocketed. Three days later, now convinced that he wanted to be a Marine, he was on his way to OCS at Quantico, Virginia.

After what he recollects to be punishing physical training, Nick became an officer. He thought of becoming a fighter pilot, but when he found that the training would require him to extend his enlistment, he changed his mind. He was initially slated to go to Korea, but in July 1953, President Dwight D. Eisenhower had brought the police action there to a close with the division of the country at the 38th parallel. Instead Nick was assigned to a Marine Battalion Landing Team stationed aboard the *U.S.S. Cambria,* a Bayfield-class attack transport.

Galifianakis became a member of a combat ready force of 700 Marines charged with keeping the peace in the Mediterranean Sea and assisting Americans in need of evacuation. Nick recalls fondly his years of service aboard the *Cambria*, in which he had the opportunity to see many of the ports in the Mediterranean either in landing exercises or on leave. The only time combat seemed a possibility was when he led a contingent of Marines to capture what were rumored to be guerillas on the island of Sardinia. The rumors were false, and the projected month's campaign was finished in a few days.

Nick on active duty.

Of all the comradery that Nick enjoyed during his time in the Marines, what stood out most was an unexpected reunion with his brother Mike and their subsequent exploration of the family's roots. When the *Cambria* called at Istanbul, Turkey, he ran into his brother, Mike, who, as a seaman, was stationed aboard an aircraft carrier, the *U.S.S. Lake Champlain*. When Nick found out that his force was scheduled to make a landing at Suda Bay on Crete, his ancestral home, he sought and obtained a temporary transfer of Mike to the *Cambria*. The brothers then obtained joint leave to visit family on the island. Galifianakis went to the PX aboard the carrier and bought cigarettes and school supplies to take to his ancestral home. The school supplies were designed for the school that their father had built just before his marriage. After the successful conclusion of the NATO exercise, the grandsons, visited their extended family who welcomed their American relatives with a feast accompanied by wine that flowed freely from the barrel.

Despite his enjoyment of his time on active duty, saying he felt guilty for taking a salary, Nick was ready to return to Durham. Not only did he have a career to build, but, as the eldest of the children, he assumed a special responsibility to take care of his family.

His years in service had not dimmed his interest in the law, and through various avenues he quickly developed his legal skills. First, he became the staff attorney with the clinic that was operated by the Duke School of Law. Its founder in 1931, John S. Bradway, was still its head, though he would retire in a few years. The clinic, one of the first established by a law school, sought to give law students some exposure to the practice of law. Galifianakis was involved in getting local attorneys to take on law students as interns to expose them to the actual practice of law. The job did not preclude Nick serving private clients whose legal problems could not be handled as part of his staff position, so he also honed his skills in the courtroom and as a counsellor.

Clinics such as the one operated by Duke were necessary because as the twentieth century progressed, practitioners were driven out of teaching positions in law schools and replaced by academics. The goal was to make the study of law a scholarly enterprise worthy of a place in an institute of higher learning. The result was graduates who could think and reason, but had little or no knowledge of law as it was practiced. Legal firms were expected, through summer clerkships or early days of full employment, to complete the practical education of law school graduates. Today all law schools have clinics, usually serving the poor or other disadvantaged groups, and practicing lawyers are often welcomed as adjunct teachers, At Duke Law School's clinic Nick was introduced both as a student and now as an instructor to a wide variety of legal matters. One other function of Duke's clinic was the teaching of legal ethics. At this time, law schools did not generally have a legal ethics course in the curriculum, and if they did, it certainly was not required. Only after the Watergate scandal in the 1970s implicated so many lawyers, did legal ethics become a required part of law school curriculums.

Also, within a year of leaving military service, Nick formed a partnership with another lawyer, Roger Upchurch. While Upchurch would restrict his practice to certain areas of the law, Galifianakis took whatever legal business came his way. In addition to working with the Duke clinic and practicing law with Upchurch, Nick served as president of the Durham Young Lawyers Club.

As the 1950s were drawing to an end, Nick began teaching a course in business law in Duke University's Department of Economics. At that time, Duke did not have a business school, and Nick's course quickly became one of the department's most popular. As Nick's course attracted more and more students, he was accused of masking his limited academic credentials with showmanship. Indeed, his effervescent personality was attractive to students. Just keeping ahead of his students, his love of learning added to the enthusiasm of his presentations. He would continue teaching these classes until 1967.

Nick as a Marine Corps captain in the reserves.

INTERLUDE 3

Practicing Law

Legal education at Duke University, as at law schools generally, was primarily focused on "book learning." Students would be expected to learn about the actual practice of law on the job or in the school's clinic. Most of the book learning, of course, was focused on the subject areas of the law, torts, contracts, constitutional law, etc. Perhaps the most important lesson that Nick took away from his legal study was the crucial importance of learning legal procedure. For instance, two lawyers might be equally knowledgeable about the substance of the law but the one who knows the mechanics of procedure will not only appear to be, but actually will be, more competent. Applying that lesson, Galifianakis quickly mastered the sometimes quirky legal procedure in all of the courts in which he practiced. The clerk of court in Durham County, who saw so many young lawyers stumble as they tried their cases, said that he was impressed with Nick's competence. The clerk conveyed this observation to Nick's father at the Lincoln Café. Teary-eyed, Mike thanked the clerk for sharing his opinion with a proud father.

As a beginning practitioner, Nick had the advantage of a Greek community that felt more comfortable discussing their legal problems with one of their own. Other lawyers would limit their practices, but from the start Galifianakis enjoyed the challenges of general practice. He felt, on principle and for the sake of his finances, that he could not be picky, so he did not turn away anyone who asked for his help. If the subject area was one with which he was not familiar, he would quickly learn all he could.

Nick did not avoid matters that involved challenging the establishment. One example involved a black client who owed a judge $100; the client's inability to pay resulted in the judge levying upon some valuable acreage that the client owned. Obviously, the land was worth much more than the value of the loan, so Nick decided to sue the judge to stop the levy. When he sought to file papers with the clerk of court in Oxford, the clerk refused to accept them on grounds that you do not sue a judge. To get the clerk to perform his administrative duty, Nick had to obtain a writ of mandamus from the superior court directing the clerk to accept the filing. Although many other lawyers would shy away from such a case, and the work it entailed, Nick was not going to let injustice triumph. Was not the purpose of a law degree to help those persons who could not help themselves?

Nick's practice of law over a lifetime would rest solidly on the base he created in his early years.

CHAPTER IV

The North Carolina Legislature: First Campaign and First Term, 1961-1963

Nick seemed born to be a political animal, but he always claimed that he only sought office at the urging of his friends and supporters. When, over a cup of coffee, a friend first suggested he run for the state legislature, Nick said that his name was enough to defeat him. (And in fact, he would be dogged throughout his political career with statements that implied that his ethnic name meant that he was not an American and certainly not a Southerner. Of course, he was arguably the best of both.) When the friend suggested that Galifianakis just test the waters by paying the $18 filing fee, Nick responded that he would not get 18 votes. The friends agreed to disagree and moved on to other topics as they finished their coffee.

Unbeknownst to Nick, though, his friend did not drop the matter and easily persuaded thirty-six of Nick's Duke University colleagues to contribute fifty cents each to pay the $18 filing fee so that Nick could run for the state house of representatives in 1960. Only on the last filing day, when all candidates had to acknowledge their candidacy, was Nick told that he would have to pay a visit to the clerk's office and fill out the necessary paperwork if the filing fee money was not to be wasted. This backward entry into politics may seem strange for a man with Nick's personality and interests, but one suspects that one way or another he would have found this particular calling. His ninth grade civics teacher had, after all, predicted that political service was in this young man's future.

Although Nick said he doubted that a candidate with a name such as Galifianakis could win political office in North Carolina, he had actually – if unknowingly –prepared well for this first attempt. Since returning from active duty with the United States Marines, he had plunged into community service of various types. He was well known at Duke, and in the city as well, through a range of charitable activities. Clearly such activity was helpful to his legal practice, but for Nick it also satisfied his need for interaction with others. He was chairman of the business division of the local American Cancer Society, a member of the board of directors of the March of Dimes, a solicitor for the United Fund, and a member of Durham's Social Planning Council. In addition, he was an active member of the Durham Junior Chamber of Commerce and the Durham County Young Democrats Club. Galifianakis won state recognition from the North Carolina Jaycees and the Durham Junior Chamber of Commerce. He also sat on the board of trustees of St. Barbara's Hellenic Church.

Finally, his armed services obligation mandated time in the reserves, which involved interaction with a wide variety of people. It was a task he undertook with his customary enthusiasm, and he became commander of the local unit on May 1, 1960. Clearly this 31-year-old man had visibility in the city and in the county.

The reason politicians have historically started small, paying their dues by initially seeking state or local office was that a political base could be created. Nick's style of politics, up close and personal, was ideally suited to local politics and to creating that base. Nick's candidacy came at an opportune time, since Watts Hill, Jr. and Ralph Strayhorn, the two representatives from Durham County, were vacating their seats in the North Carolina General Assembly's House of Representatives, thus opening up the political race. Nick became the third announced candidate in the Democratic Party primary for the House seat. He ran an ad in the Durham papers emphasizing his achievements and stressing the fact that he was born and educated in Durham.

In 1960 and today, North Carolina's General Assembly consists of a House and a Senate. The House has 120 members with at least one from each of the state's 100 counties, the more populous having additional representatives. The Senate has 50 members and is more proportionately based with voting districts generally combining counties. For his house district, Galifianakis would be running against two opponents and would have to outpoll one of them. The way the primary system worked for the state house was that the two highest vote-getters would become the Democratic candidates. To become one of the top two, it was apparent early in the campaign that Nick should pay a visit to Judge Noyes Hight. Judge was a nickname, not a title, and he was always nattily dressed and easy to find in the lobby of the Washington Duke Hotel. Rumor had it that Hight had been put on a lifetime retainer for having served time for a crime that the payer of the retainer had committed. Hight therefore did not have to concern himself with making a living and could offer his opinions and knowledge of the state to whomever he liked. He had a reputation for picking political winners. At their first meeting, he told Nick that winning the primary was simply not possible, given the fact that the two other candidates came from well-established political families. But, as with so many others, Hight took a liking to Nick and became a volunteer political advisor. He told Nick he had to go out into the rural areas of the district and get acquainted with the people who lived there. Following that advice, while he was out in Carr Township, Nick ran across a man on a tractor and introduced himself. Bob Cook, the man on the tractor, happened to be more influential than his overalls conveyed, and although he wouldn't know it at the time, Nick had that day garnered much more than a single farmer's vote.

One morning not long after Nick's encounter with Cook, Hight called Nick at 4:30 a.m. and suggested that he quickly dress and meet the tobacco workers as they changed shifts. Nick, who often saw himself following the dictates of others, dutifully complied. Not only did he introduce himself to the workers, but he also plied them with candy, making himself memorable. The episode led Nick to coin the first of the many slogans that would become a regular part of his political campaigns: "Sweets to the Sweet." Clearly the slogan was more appropriate in his campaign for female votes, but the candy itself appealed to both sexes.

In this first race for public office Nick Galifianakis, along with the assistance of Judge Hight, developed a pattern for political campaigning that he would employ into the future. It was deeply personal. He relied, usually quite successfully, on the proposition that if a person got to know him he would have that person's support. It was not a matter of ego as much as it was taking advantage of a personality that turned strangers into friends. For Nick, this style of campaigning was second nature and would pay off.

The only political veteran in the three-man Democratic Party primary race was Henry Godwin who had run unsuccessfully in 1958. His experience served him no better this time, as Nick led the ticket with 13,255 votes. Eugene C. Brooks, III gained the second nomination. There was no Republican opposition in the general election, meaning that the victors in the Democratic primary were assured victory in November. Nick was reputed to be the first Greek-American elected to any state legislature in the Southeastern United States and certainly one of the youngest, at 31, to serve in the state's General Assembly. When informed of this historic milestone, he indicated that he was elected to represent the interests of all of Durham County's citizens. Although Galifianakis warmly and publicly embraced his Greek heritage and the Greek Orthodox religion, he did not like being called a Greek-American. He was simply an American. Elated by the victory, he wrote to Judge Hight, saying "I will always be grateful to you for your guidance, for your interest, and for your consideration for a candidate who did not know which end was up."

Being a legislator in North Carolina was a part-time job with a legislative session scheduled once a term (every two years), but with additional special sessions possible at the governor's pleasure. Galifianakis, as all members, was paid a $15 daily salary with a $12 per diem for living expenses, as well as actual travel based on mileage, including one round trip home each week. Nick continued to teach his business law course in the Department of Economics at Duke and to practice law in Durham during his time in the General Assembly.

Nick would be no bashful first-year representative in the 1961 session. He got acquainted with both his colleagues and the support staff. Galifianakis quickly established himself as a legislator to watch, and his engaging personality inevitably drew attention. Perhaps more importantly, Nick applied the lesson he had learned as a lawyer: that knowing *how* to proceed with legal matters was of critical importance, something that seemed obvious but was often neglected. From very early in his legal practice, Galifianakis mastered the rules of legal procedure. Now in Raleigh, he studied the process by which laws were made, taking on himself the task of drafting the bills he brought forward. From his first term in the General Assembly, when many of his colleagues were concentrating their attention on how much of the old racially segregated South could be saved, Galifianakis was looking forward to a different future.

Improvement in the state's public education system was high on Governor Terry Sanford's agenda, and Nick concurred, arguing that increased funding was an investment in North Carolina's future. Furthermore, he agreed that education was the coming legislative session's "chief business." Galifianakis said that he did not favor any new taxes but would await arguments to the contrary. He noted that the state ranked 44th in public school expenditure, only $230 per pupil, well below the national average of $369. Rather than increase taxes to meet educational needs, Nick suggested that the state should work to attract industry and take advantage of the state's ports. What disturbed Galifianakis most was the proposed sales tax on food. When Nick suggested substituting a tax on cigarettes, Sanford told him that was politically impossible. In the final analysis, Nick finally concluded that a new tax was necessary and supported the governor's proposal to levy an across-the-board sales tax of 3%. Of course now in many states, including North Carolina, there is a tiered sales tax system, allowing food to be taxed at a lower rate.

He also saw the need for reapportioning the state's electoral districts, saying that the legislature should heed its own constitutional provisions that had long been ignored rather than wait for the Supreme Court decision in *Baker v. Carr,* a case from Tennessee. (The case challenged the state's failure to take into account population changes since 1900 in the apportionment of seats in its legislature.) Also in his first term, Nick argued that innovative programs to improve highway safety in the state were needed. Except for reapportionment, which would inevitably reduce rural influence in the legislature, Nick seemed to be on relatively safe political ground. And even on reapportionment, Durham County was becoming less and less rural. However, to allay fears, he did promote rural North Carolina interests by supporting farm agencies and working for funds to improve rural roads. Clearly he was beginning his political career by trying to steer clear of controversial matters.

Nick gained a visibility usually denied freshmen legislators in large part because of his willingness to talk to reporters. One might even say, to paraphrase Will Rogers, that he never met a reporter he did not like. Galifianakis' tendency to stay at his desk after the House chamber cleared made him accessible to reporters who were then allowed to come on the floor. Nick's affability and willingness to respond to their inquiries made him a press favorite. For instance, he charmed reporter Aurora Dolley, whose profile of Nick ran in several state papers in March of 1961. She began her piece by saying that if it were considered work to interview "personable young legislators like Nick Galifianakis," then she would endorse minimum wages for maximum hours. For her interview, Dolley said, she not only had to elbow out legislators who wanted to talk with the freshman representative but also "the flock of pagettes so attentive to the young bachelor." She noted that his charm and intellect were complimented by "a somewhat overwhelming smile." Finally, several paragraphs in, the reporter began to write of Nick's upbringing and the issues that concerned him as a legislator.

Joe Hunt, the House Speaker in 1961, put Nick on the Appropriations Committee, the Committee on Mental

Institutions, and the House Judiciary I Committee. As a member of the Appropriations Committee, Nick was often approached to initiate requests for funding certain state projects. For instance, the buildings at Bennett Place, the location of the surrender of the largest number of Confederate troops seventeen days after Appomattox, had fallen into disrepair and $15,000 was needed to complete their reconstruction. Nick successfully steered the request through the House. He did no less when the Pulitzer prize winning playwright Paul Green sought support for the summertime performances of his outdoor drama, a groundbreaking play called *The Lost Colony*. When Green told Nick that the project badly needed an infusion of dollars to survive, Nick, to the delight of Green, said he would sponsor a bill providing the money.

Outside of his legislative duties, Nick also took the lead, as chair of the 14th Judicial Bar Association Legal Aid Committee, to propose a five-step program to put a legal aid clinic into operation. Nick had worked with the clinic established at the Duke Law School, and he now recommended that the city of Durham meet its obligation of providing equal access to legal services. Nick added that law students could help staff the clinic and in the process gain valuable practical experience. He estimated that a budget of $8,500 would cover the costs for the first year of operation.

So Nick's first term was busy and fulfilling, and he did not need his friends to pay the filing fee for his re-election bid when his two-year term was up.

The election in 1962 saw Galifianakis and Brooks again emerging victorious in the Democratic primary, with Nick repeating his success as the leading vote getter. A black candidate had challenged the incumbents, but without the endorsement of the Durham Committee on Negro Affairs, he ran a poor third. In the general election the sole Republican candidate was outpolled by both Galifianakis and Brooks by over a three to one count.

Not long after his reelection, on April 5, 1963, Nick gave up his bachelor status and married a woman whom he had been dating, Louise Cheatham Ruggles. They were married at St. Barbara's Greek Orthodox Church in Durham with Nick's brother, Mike, as his best man. The couple had met at a bachelors and spinsters Christmas party five years earlier when neither was thinking of marriage—Louise because of her recent divorce, and Nick because of his obligation to see that his brothers were educated. One of Nick's high school classmates had escorted Louise to the party, and he resented the attention Galifianakis was paying her. Louise did not immediately warm to Nick's overtures, but after a number of telephone conversations she began to accept his courtship. She brought to their marriage a nine-year old daughter, Stephanie, whom Nick adopted. Together they would have two children, Katherine, born in 1964 and Jon Mark born in 1966.

The 1963 session of the General Assembly was the first to meet in the new State Legislative Building. What absorbed much of the legislature's attention was a reapportionment proposal called the "Little Federal Plan" that did not equitably distribute seats. Under its provisions, House membership would be reduced from 120 to 100 with each county having equal representation, and the Senate would be expanded from 50 to 70 with new senatorial districts created that could vary in population by as much as 25%. Galifianakis, who believed that the plan did not meet the objections to the present allocation of seats, was credited with getting the Durham delegation to oppose it.

Reapportionment was a hot topic because in *Baker v. Carr* in 1962, the United States Supreme Court had served notice on the states that the apportionment of seats in their legislatures was in all likelihood unconstitutional because it counted the votes of some voters more than others. Over the next two terms, the Justices clarified the equal protection requirement by establishing the standard of "one person, one vote." That standard required that each house of the state legislature represent all persons equally, meaning that each voting district should contain approximately the same population. States had counties of widely varying population and giving each county the same representation meant that the weight of a vote in a lightly populated county counted much more than one cast in a densely populated county. Some states resisted, citing the fact that such plans took the United States Senate as the model. Each state, despite the vast differences in population, had two senators. The Supreme Court rejected the analogy, saying that the obvious malapportionment of the United States Senate was the result of a necessary compromise. As the Constitution was being drafted in 1787, small states wanted equal representation in the new government and large states wanted proportional representation. The so-called Grand Compromise, providing for equal representation in the Senate and proportional representation in the House of Representatives, saved the constitutional convention in Philadelphia from dissolution. Nick had apparently realized that the federal analogy would not work once the Court undertook to evaluate state apportionment under the aegis of the Fourteenth Amendment's requirement of equality. When the legislature sent the Little Federal Plan to the people in a referendum in 1964, it was decisively defeated. Galifianakis also opposed the state joining other states in calling for a constitutional convention to allow some variance in one house of the legislature. He wisely worried that such a convention could not be confined solely to the issue of reapportionment.

One of Galifianakis' legislative achievements of the new term stemmed from his chairmanship of the Committee on Mental Institutions, a leadership post he had assumed in the 1963 session. He was appalled at the conditions in which individuals were held, and he worked to humanize the caretaking. With his urging, a new State Department of Mental Health was established as well as a new program to minister to the needs of retarded (the name used at the time) blind children in the state. He was also a member of a dozen House committees, including Highway Safety, Insurance, the Judiciary, and Conservation and Development.

Nick was also instrumental in providing for the growth of the Research Triangle Park, which had been established in 1959 with 4,400 acres. Traversing two counties, Durham and Wake, it was seen as an engine for economic growth in a state with negative economic trends. With three major universities, the University of North Carolina at Chapel Hill, North Carolina State University, and Duke University, within easy reach, the idea was to tap the human resources they provided. Leaders in government, business, and academia grasped a future in which an economy based on education, science, medicine, and technology would displace one centered on tobacco, textiles, and furniture.

To be successful, the Park had to intrude upon a number of political jurisdictions, each with its own agenda, and gain the support of their local leaders. An infrastructure had to be built, and that was the first of Galifianakis' contributions to the Park's future success. He and Brooks, his fellow Durham representative, joined with representatives from neighboring counties to introduce a bill to authorize city and county governments "to act jointly in providing water and sewage facilities to population and industrial areas outside city limits." Nick said that the law would facilitate the growth of the Research Triangle Park. The Triangle already had the brain power from the universities in the area; this new legislation would deliver the utility services for the area to develop and grow. Growth would be slow prior to 1965, but in that year IBM committed to build a facility and the federal government decided to locate the National Institute of Environmental Health Sciences in the Park. The future was now assured and the Research Triangle Park was on its way to becoming the largest in the nation.

Nick's interest did not end with this contribution to the infrastructure of the park, for he was instrumental in the creation of a new center in the Park. Galifianakis asked the State Board of Education to consider establishing a scientific and technological institute in the Research Triangle Park. He suggested making the institute part of a proposed state community college program. Its primary purpose would be to train people who would be able to staff the needs of research organizations that would locate in the Park.

Not only was the North Carolina Board of Science and Technology established but within a few years it had realized its purpose: "to help the Tarheel state contribute to and reap the benefits from the economic and technical advancements in the Age of Space." Staff were hired, contracts were awarded, and land purchased for a building. Nick Galifianakis served as one of the House members on the State Board of Science and Technology. (Oddly, although Nick paved the way for new technology, he, himself, was a reluctant personal adopter of it. He resists reliance on cell phones and computers even today.)

Nick also played a significant role in the development of the state's community college system. A study in 1952 had outlined the need for community colleges, but it took five more years for the legislature to pass the Community College Act. The legislation authorized the establishment of such junior colleges under the direction of the State Board of Higher Education (now the Board of Governors of the University of North Carolina.) Over the next six years, five community colleges were established, in Wilmington, Elizabeth City, Asheville, and two in Charlotte. In 1963 a sixth college was added in Dallas. Today North Carolina has fifty-eight such institutions, making it the third largest system in the United States. A companion effort at the same time resulted in the establishment of industrial education centers. Eighteen had been created by 1961 to provide post high school education. A commission, appointed by Governor Terry Sanford, studied the situation and recommended combining the community colleges and industrial education centers, thus joining all the state's two-year programs, whether academic, vocational or technical, under one comprehensive community college system. When the legislature got this recommendation, Nick was a leader in convincing the House to meld the two programs under a Department of Community Colleges, which was created in July, 1963. The new legislation provided "for the establishment, organization, and administration of a system of educational institutions throughout the state . . . to serve as a legislative Charter for such institutions, and to authorize the levying of local taxes and the issuing of local bonds for the support thereof."

Of the six extant community colleges, three were now made four-year colleges and the remaining three were combined with twenty industrial education centers. The next major change came in 1979, long after Nick had left the state legislature. However, he viewed with pride the way in which higher education had expanded in the state to meet the challenges of a future that necessitated far more than a high school diploma.

In addition to providing for the expansion of community colleges in the state, Galifianakis sponsored two bills that provided new educational opportunities for high school students. The first one created a School of the Arts, a high school specializing in dance, drama, music, film, as well as the visual arts. It would open in Winston-Salem in 1965. The second bill created a Governor's School, located at Salem College, also in Winston Salem. Each year gifted high school students were assembled for a five-and-a-half week summer session.

These achievements in which Nick was a major player might have received more public attention had the 1963 session not ended with the hurried passage of a most controversial law.

INTERLUDE 4

Walking the Walk

In early 1963 the Durham delegation to the General Assembly was especially concerned that the State Highway Commission was ignoring a pressing need for completing a forty-mile stretch in the interstate highway system from Henderson to Durham, the only missing link on the route from Richmond, Virginia to Atlanta, Georgia. The affected area's population was growing, and the congestion resulting from a four-lane highway narrowing to two lanes over this long stretch was dangerous. Nick said he would check on the Commission's plans. When the Commission admitted that the completion of the Henderson to Durham link was more than a decade away, Nick said that was unacceptable. It was one of the many episodes in which his talk got him an inordinate amount of publicity. His constant complaints led one fellow legislator to say "If he really wants to do something about it, why doesn't he walk the damn thing." Nick replied that "If that's what it takes, that's what I'll do."

Accepting the challenge on Saturday, February 23, 1963, he began at Henderson at 9:45 a.m. with local politicians and interested onlookers wishing him well. He developed blisters early in the walk and did get some treatment, along with lunch, in Oxford. As a result of blisters and a sore toe and muscles, he accepted rides along the way, but he walked a total of about nineteen miles. He strode into Durham at 5:35 p.m. There, he was greeted by Durham mayor E. J. Evans, state Senator Claude Currie and Chamber of Commerce president Wesley Lewis, who had walked along with him for a while. They gave him a bottle of rubbing compound and some foot pads. As Nick pointed out dangerous conditions along the way, support for changing the agenda of the Highway Commission grew. Galifianakis arranged a meeting with State Highway Commission Chairman Merrill Evans for the following week.

Nick receiving the rubbing compound for his feet from Wesley Lewis with Claude Currie and E.J. Evans watching.

The publicity that accompanied Nick putting his feet where his mouth was resulted in the reordering of highway priorities. The two segments of I-85 would be linked by the end of the decade. An envious Governor Sanford called Nick and said "Hell, if I had known you were going to get this kind of publicity, I'd have walked it myself."

CHAPTER V

The North Carolina Legislature:
Two More Campaigns and Terms, 1963-1966

As the 1963 session was in its final throes, the legislature hastily passed a measure that would plague the state for most of the remaining years of the decade. The bill proposing the infamous Speaker Ban Law was introduced in the North Carolina House by Representatives Phil Godwin of Gates County and Ned Delamar of Pamlico County. The law would require all colleges or universities in the state that received any state funds to deny to the following persons the use of their facilities "for speaking purposes:" a member of the Communist Party; a person who advocates the overthrow of the Constitution; or a person invoking the Fifth Amendment to refuse to answer questions relating to subversion or Communist connections.

Godwin said in support that "We are not going to let these sort of people ply their trade in our State-supported colleges." Normal procedural rules were suspended and the bill was deemed passed in the House. A little more discussion took place in the Senate. Senate leader Clarence Stone, who had suffered a number of legislative defeats as a states-rights segregationist, rammed the bill through on a voice vote. He had witnessed how extended debate tended to defeat proposals close to his heart, therefore he decided that he would now curtail debate on this issue. Why, he undoubtedly thought, should anyone oppose denying a forum on University property to those who would destroy our democratic institutions? Since North Carolina at that time did not give its governor veto power, the passage of the bill through both houses made it law.

Nick Galifianakis sought to explain why such a law was not only undesirable but unconstitutional as well, but with little success among the majority of his colleagues. For the strong stand that he took, he received plaudits from Bill Friday, the president of the University of North Carolina system, William C. Archie, the Director of the State Board of Education, Michael H. Lawler, president of the student body at the University in Chapel Hill, and John C. Brooks, a researcher at the North Carolina Supreme Court, among others. Brooks said that Nick's "courageous" stand against the pressures "exerted by those who would restrict the flow of ideas . . . . [exemplified] the highest personal and political character."

When the law was reported the following day educational leaders in the state protested and asked that the legislature repeal the hastily enacted legislation. The Senate had a procedure whereby a bill that had been passed could be recalled, but the attempt failed by a 19-35 count. Thirteen senators insisted that their protest be put into the Senate Journal. Galifianakis led the House in following suit, as fourteen representatives signed a similar statement. The gist of the protest was that the Speaker Ban Law denied free speech, something especially precious in a learning environment.

The capital city newspaper the *News & Observer* lent its editorial voice to the opposition. It was especially incensed when the North Carolina Attorney General T. Wade Bruton denied that the law was unconstitutional, saying that the state could regulate state property with full discretion. The newspaper in an editorial headed "'Is an Ass,'" alluding to Charles Dickens's description of the law, labeled

Bruton an out-of-date ass.

By the early 1960s, the worry about domestic communist influence had largely dissipated, but in the South many politicians had long characterized the civil rights crusade as a communist plot. In an infamous Senate race in 1950, the appointed incumbent, Frank Porter Graham, plucked from his position as president of the University of North Carolina to fill a vacant seat, had been defeated by accusations that he supported communists and favored racial equality. When the United States Supreme Court began to chip away at racial segregation and then attack the system in public schools, many white Southerners were incensed at this interference in their long-established social system. Resistance was the order of the day.

As the new law demonstrated, the anticommunist stance still seemed to play well in North Carolina long after it had lost political clout elsewhere. Four days before the passage of the Speaker Ban Law, Jesse Helms, a radio and television commentator, whose editorials were beamed to listeners on the Tobacco Network and often printed in newspapers in the eastern part of the state, had praised Ohio's consideration of similar legislation and said it provided a lesson for those "who have been too timid, or too disinterested, or both, to take a stand." Helms had focused on the University in Chapel Hill, convinced that the school was providing a forum for communists, who sought the destruction of freedom in part by "poisoning the intellectual climate and the educational system." He continually lumped together his opposition to civil rights and to much of American foreign policy with his fear of communism and his hatred of liberalism. The passage of the North Carolina law, Helms editorialized, was just what the Chapel Hill campus needed.

While many of the rural inhabitants of eastern North Carolina applauded Helms' stand, the University administrators, believing that repeal was unlikely, began to argue for modification of the law. The law, they said, was too inclusive in that it ensnared both speakers who had much to contribute to the educational environment and artistic performers. Furthermore, the law might well threaten the accreditation of the institutions. The chancellor of the University at Chapel Hill was William B. Aycock, who had recently given notice that he would step down and return to teaching in the law school. Aycock took a forceful position against the law and garnered support from both within and outside the academic community. The president of the multi-campus University of North Carolina system, the recently installed William C. Friday, also opposed the law and sought its modification, but, unlike Aycock, he was more circumspect in his opposition.

Controversy percolated over the next two years, and although all 1964 Democratic gubernatorial candidates, I. Beverly Lake, L. Richardson Preyer and Dan K. Moore, supported the law and ignored Chancellor Aycock's arguments, the winner would have to contend with a controversy that was injuring the state's reputation. The winner in the governor's race was Moore, and he had been informed by the Southern Association of Colleges and Schools that the law interfered with academic freedom and placed the accreditation of the state institutions of higher learning in jeopardy. In the regular session of the legislature in 1965, General Assembly members were waiting for Moore to take a position on the matter. Worried about their political future, they believed that they would be protected if the governor said that change was necessary.

In late June 1965, with accreditation concerns looming,

Governor Moore appointed a study commission to make recommendations concerning the law. The Southern Association for Colleges and Schools, the accrediting agency, was meeting in late November, and if the commission moved quickly and came up with a recommendation a special session of the legislature could be called to enact the change before that meeting. Former chancellor Aycock testified before the committee and summoned the words of the enthusiastic backer of the law Jesse Helms in support of the principle of free speech. A year earlier WRAL, the Raleigh television station that carried Helms' editorials, had been challenged under the then prevailing fairness doctrine applied by the Federal Communications Commission. Helms took to the air to condemn such government-imposed censorship, saying "when one is denied any part of his rightful freedom, then every man's freedom has been lessened." Aycock said he heartily agreed with Helms.

After hearings, the FCC recommended a plan that would place on the boards of trustees of the respective campuses of the University system the full responsibility for developing and implementing a policy that would determine who should speak on campus, distinguishing between those who would contribute to the education of students versus those who would serve to advance the cause of the nation's enemies. Governor Moore, claiming that the proposal had found a "middle ground" between the two sides, said he supported the change "both in letter and spirit." Apparently this gubernatorial blessing provided members of the legislature with the cover they needed to vote for the law's modification. Nick, in anticipation of the special session meeting on November 15th, expected the legislature to go along with the recommendation. He hoped it would be done quickly so that the matter of redistricting could then be tackled.

Steadfast supporters of the original law could do little to save it, but they did vote against the amendment, the House vote being 75 to 39 in favor of the amendment and the Senate vote 36 to 13. Governor Moore's hope that the compromise would end the controversy was too optimistic. But, since the new law left the boards of trustees with the responsibility to "adopt and publish regulations governing the use of facilities...for speaking purposes," the Southern Association for Colleges and Schools was satisfied and the threat to accreditation disappeared. However, by designating the individuals earlier banned as "dangerous," the trustees of the various institutions were expected to deny a forum to certain individuals, and so they did under the amended law.

Although the administrators of the specially targeted campus in Chapel Hill thought that they could live with the compromise, other persons disagreed and sought the law's repeal. Well after Nick had left the state legislature, a three judge federal court on February 19, 1968 invalidated the law and its enforcement procedures as "facially unconstitutional because of vagueness." The revised law of 1965 was declared "null and void." The court did not hesitate, however, to endorse the anticommunist crusade. Despite the personal sympathy of the judges, the law just could not be squared with the constitutional protection of free speech.

Galifianakis' opposition to the enactment of the Speaker Ban Law would be cited in his subsequent electoral campaigns as evidence of his being soft on communism, an argument that because of the linkage of communism and civil rights would continue to resonate with North Carolina voters.

Nick's second term in the General Assembly had been

even more productive and newsworthy than his first, and in part because of that record, on February 11, 1964 he was honored by the Junior Chamber of Commerce as the Outstanding Young Man of the Year. The award was presented by Douglas Knight, the president of Duke University.

Nick receiving the award with Bob Westbrook, his campaign manager.

Galifianakis enjoyed serving in the legislature and stood for election for a third term in 1965. Having polled the highest number of votes cast for local officials in the last two elections, he was fairly confident of success. He was thankful for the confidence the voters had placed in him and said he wanted to continue with projects in the areas of education, roads, health, and science and technology. Nick, in announcing his candidacy, said: "North Carolina is on the threshold of a new era and I want to do all I can do to enhance that development." Again a single Republican, this time Oliver W. Alphin, appeared on the general election ballot in November, but Nick and the other Democrat, Hance Hofler, easily outpolled the challenger. Nick had his eye on higher political office, but for the present he felt he needed to continue to amass a record that would show that he had not only paid his dues but had also distinguished himself as an active and concerned legislator.

The 126th session of the North Carolina General Assembly that convened on February 3. 1965 contained six women, five in the House and one in the Senate. In 1964 the voters had approved a state constitutional amendment to equalize property rights between men and women. Now Nick, with the enthusiastic support of his female colleagues, introduced eleven bills to carry out the purpose of the amendment.

As chairman of the House Judiciary Committee, Nick wanted members who would be willing to work as hard as he did, and he did not hesitate to reach across the aisle to the opposing party. For instance, Nick was successful in getting the House speaker Pat Taylor to appoint Republican Jim Holshouser to the committee. For this action, Galifianakis was taken to task by members of his own party, but he stood firm, contending that competence and commitment bested party affiliation.

In other business, when the House sought to put the legislature on record as calling for a constitutional convention to overturn the Supreme Court's recent ruling requiring reapportionment, Nick tried to head off the decision, still worried that such a convention would be bound by no limits. With assistance, he was successful in bringing the matter back for further study, but this maneuver only delayed the inevitable. The House voted 95-23 in favor of the resolution. Twenty-one states had already passed a similar measure. Eventually the campaign would fail, coming up short of the thirty-four states required to call such a convention. Nick was still concerned that his fellow legislators had no real desire to deal with the matter of reapportionment. He worried that the issue would be handled by the courts should the legislature not address the matter in a timely fashion.

For moral and business reasons, Nick opposed a proposed resolution to condemn Martin Luther King's attempt to economically boycott the state of Alabama because of its resistance to integration. Galifianakis argued that the resolution could produce "problems that this state has not had." He proudly proclaimed that the state "leads the South in race relations," and therefore opposed a measure that might well undermine that most desirable status. Perhaps opposition to such a resolution was not politically harmful in 1965, but Nick understood that supporting Governor Dan Moore's proposal to enact a motor vehicle inspection law might be politically costly. An inspection law had been passed in 1947 but then repealed in 1949 after much public protest over inspection procedures. Nick felt the new law eliminated the inconvenience of the old by providing that any service station or garage was empowered to provide the inspection. He sought to counter the political liability by arguing that what is politically safe must defer to the fact that peoples' lives were at stake, something that he felt must trump any political consideration. The measure eventually passed easily.

One matter high on Nick's personal agenda when he came to the legislature in 1961 was reform of the state's judiciary. Lawyers in the state were well aware of the sorry state of the North Carolina court system. At the time the state financed the Supreme Court and the superior courts, but local courts were established and supported only by cities and counties where they were located. This situation resulted in different courts and different judicial procedures depending upon where you found yourself within the state. Furthermore, much of the administration of justice, both civil and criminal, had been left to justices of the peace, and clerks of the superior court, all of whom were paid on a fee basis. To make matters even worse, some justices of the peace only received fees if a person was found guilty of the crime charged. Attempts to standardize the system failed in 1959 because reform required a change in the state constitution, and the three-fifths vote needed for the legislature to submit the proposal to voters in the next general election could not be mustered. Governor Luther Hodges had suggested that the North Carolina Bar study the problem and come up with recommendations. At the same time, the General Assembly created a constitutional commission to look at the problem. Both groups came in with similar recommendations—establish an all-inclusive court system uniform throughout the state and paid for by the state.

Speaker Pat Taylor now took the lead and asked Nick and Gus Zollicuffer to line up the votes. As a leading advocate for reform of the court system, Nick readily accepted and worked to achieve the result that he had long desired. The constitutional amendment required for change in the judiciary had been ratified by the voters, and now in 1965 comprehensive legislation centralized a court structure that did away with the myriad local courts in favor of a single district court. That court would now divide jurisdiction with the other trial court, the superior court. The office of justice of the peace was abolished and in its place the office of magistrate was created. All was to be state financed under an Administrative Office of the Courts which would direct the non-judicial affairs, the administrative and business part of the judicial branch. The enabling legislation was introduced by Nick and others to put this new plan into operation in stages. By 1970 all the thirty judicial districts would have district courts. In 1967, the General Assembly passed legislation in accordance with a constitutional amendment ratified by the voters in 1965 to create an appellate tier of courts to reduce the burden upon the state supreme court. That completed the organization of the state judiciary as it exists in North Carolina today.

Despite his many successes in getting what he considered necessary legislation through the House, Galifianakis was frustrated by his failure in two other matters that had occupied his attention from his arrival in Raleigh. The first and more difficult task was raising the state income tax exemption for dependents from $300 to $600. What made the change difficult was the apparent need for a constitutional amendment giving the General Assembly the power to make such changes. Many state constitutions, including North Carolina's, out of a distrust of the legislature, required a two-step process for certain changes in the law: first a submission of the change to the people in the form of a constitutional amendment, and then legislative action. Nick's bill in the 1965 session had twenty-eight co-sponsors, indicating that the Durham representative was making some headway in convincing his colleagues. Opponents said the $11,000,000 that would be lost in revenue was more than the state could bear. Nick responded, saying that the money individual taxpayers saved would be spent, thereby replacing what had been lost from the income tax with increased revenue from the sales tax. Eventually in 1969, after Nick had left the General Assembly, it submitted the amendment to the electorate, and by the time 1970 state income tax returns were filed the personal exemption for dependents had been raised to the $600 Nick had desired.

The second piece of unfinished business concerned his failure to bring daylight saving time to the state. A positive vote in the House was getting closer as the 2-1 negative margin in the 1961 session, dwindled to 6-5 in 1965. As chairman of the Judiciary I Committee, he cited the heavy volume of mail urging the enactment of daylight saving time in the state. By a nine to one margin the people of the state had indicated their support. Nick fought hard to deliver what the people wanted, but he had been unsuccessful. Eventually, the majority of North Carolinians would finally get what they wanted through the action of Congress. The Federal Uniform Time Act of 1966 mandated daylight saving time throughout the nation beginning April 30, 1967. A state could exempt itself from the operation of the act by formal action of its legislature. Although some members of the North Carolina General Assembly sought an exemption, they, now, were unsuccessful. So, daylight saving time advocates had not their representatives in Raleigh to thank but the United States Congress instead. The very federal government that many state residents saw as a threat to the ability of the state to manage its own affairs was now the majority's savior.

Despite the seriousness of the matters before the legislature in the mid-1960s and his own heavy workload, Galifianakis, with his quick wit and predilection for puns, rarely passed up an opportunity to have some fun. For instance, when William C. McIntire, Jr., executive secretary of the North Carolina Bakers Association, one day deposited sixteen donuts on every seat in the General Assembly and every desk in the newsroom, Nick could not resist commenting. He had his secretary send a letter to McIntire that read as follows: "Dear Breadman: "Thanks a 'hole' lot for the sweet bread."

As the 1965 session of the legislature was winding down, there were matters that had to be addressed before the next regular session. Not one but two special sessions were called, one dealing with the amendment to the Speaker Ban Law and the other dealing with reapportionment of voting districts.

Nick had served three two-year terms in the General Assembly, encompassing three regular sessions and three special sessions. He had honed his legislative skills and was satisfied with what he had accomplished. He was especially pleased with the role he had played in reforming the state court system, establishing the Research Triangle Park, and laying the basis for community college growth in the state. These achievements forecast a future that he urged his fellow North Carolinians to embrace. Reporters and political observers came to see the man from Durham as a new breed of politician, one who put the stultifying past behind in favor of summoning new opportunities for future growth and accomplishment. Taking issue with the lyrics of the old southern song *Dixie*, Nick wanted to show that old times *could* be forgotten.

The accomplishment of so many of his goals, coupled with the reapportionment of the voting districts that the second special legislative session produced, paved the way for Nick to finally consider a run for Congress..

Nick with Governor Sanford and Durham mayor E.J. Evans and his wife.

INTERLUDE 5

Walter Cronkite Takes Notice of Some Legislative Hijinks

Because he worked hard at it, Nick was well-versed in the procedures of the law-making process, and new members of the General Assembly did not hesitate to take advantage of the easily approached veteran legislator. One such episode stands out from the rest. In May of 1965, Macon County's lone representative in the North Carolina House of Representatives, William "Bill" G. Zickgraf complained to Nick that in his first three months in the General Assembly he had not passed a single law. Galifianakis, who saw in the new arrival a resemblance to the comic strip character Li'l Abner, said representatives did not pass laws, but that they could propose them. Zickgraf said then that is what he wanted to do. When he could not come up with a subject, Nick, who had been looking through the statutes to find outmoded or unenforced provisions that should be repealed, suggested that Bill propose the repeal of a provision in an 1802 law prescribing the death penalty for the survivor of a duel in which his adversary was killed. Galifianakis said there was a conflict of the law with the state constitution in that the constitution listed the crimes for which the death penalty could be levied, and that section did not include death as the result of a duel. The law had gone largely unenforced in the state before the Civil War, and after the conflict it was an anachronism. Galifianakis, who drafted all his own bills, despite the availability of staff support, formulated the proposal and briefed the Macon County representative on its presentation to the House.

Zickgraf insisted that Nick be a co-sponsor of the proposed legislation. Nick agreed, but it was understood that Zickgraf would present the bill for the House's approval at a Monday night session open to the public. Then, Bill's friends and relatives could be present to see their representative at work. What followed was what one House colleague referred to as the "Nick and Zick show." At the Monday night session, Speaker Pat Taylor called upon Zickgraff to explain the bill and its justification. Looking at the microphone, the nervous representative froze and then yielded the floor to the bill's co-sponsor, Nick Galifianakis. Nick made the required presentation, and then moved that a vote be taken, and by voice vote the bill passed. A House colleague had contributed swords to the evening spectacle, and the bill's co-sponsors each took a sword as they playfully dueled, moving from the House to the Senate. There the bill was also immediately passed by a voice vote, thus removing the old provision. After the evening's performance, both houses adjourned.

The next day as Walter Cronkite ended his CBS Evening News broadcast, he said: "If you want to duel, go to North Carolina where you no longer can be put to death for dueling. And that's the way it is."

CHAPTER VI

Aiming for Congress: The First Primary, 1966

As early as his first year in Raleigh, attentive ears heard rumors that Nick Galifianakis would run for Congress. Since the state in 1965 was redistricting pursuant to a court order, Nick had a special interest in how the map would look and where his home county of Durham would be placed. Nick might have mounted a successful challenge to Horace R. Kornegay, who represented Durham in the 6th Congressional district, but a number of plans severed Durham from Guilford County, Kornegay's home district. To deal with reapportionment the legislature was called into special session on November 15. Failing to reach agreement before the holidays, it convened again on January 10, 1966.

On the eve of the special session, a joint legislative committee proposed joining Durham with Forsyth County, where Winston-Salem was located. The Durham Chamber of Commerce passed a resolution opposing the joinder and threatening court action if its sentiments were ignored. The *Winston-Salem Journal* said that the placing of Durham County "has probably caused more behind-the-scenes maneuvering and political talk than any other aspect of redistricting." Would-be candidates for Congress from this newly proposed district, including Nick Galifianakis, were careful not to say anything to offend voters in either of the two counties. However, the Winston-Salem Chamber of Commerce State and Local Government Committee, not to be outdone, also protested Forsyth's inclusion in a district with Durham County. Despite the opposition, the joinder happened and the new 5th District was created. Fortunately for candidates seeking to represent the new 5th District, it had no incumbent since Ralph J. Scott, who was from Stokes County, decided not to seek re-election.

Along with Galifianakis, Smith W. Bagley, heir to a tobacco fortune, and William "Bill" Z. Wood, both of Forsyth County, were mentioned as likely candidates. Although Nick would have preferred that Forsyth County not be joined with Durham, he did find support for his candidacy among his fellow legislators in the special session. Another entrant into the race was Harold Thomerson, but he was also from Winston-Salem, leaving Nick the only candidate from Durham County. The new district also contained Person, Caswell, Rockingham and Stokes counties, and it stretched for 100 miles. The district met the one man-one vote standard, but it certainly was far from compact, a requirement added by a three-judge federal court.

Durham had been added to the 5th District not to attract any candidate but simply to provide sufficient population for a man from Winston-Salem to fill the seat vacated by Scott. That man was Smith Bagley, a relative newcomer to the state, a deficiency compensated for by being the grandson of R. J. Reynolds, the tobacco giant. At thirty-one, Bagley was a handsome man standing six feet five inches tall. He had graduated from Washington & Lee College and had no prior legislative experience. The *Greensboro Record* noted that three of the candidates, all but Thomerson, who was expected to carry on Scott's conservative voting, would give the district a liberal representative for the first time.

Nick had paid his political dues and was widely regarded as an effective legislator. On the basis of his prior legislative work for the past six years in the General Assembly, he was clearly the most qualified candidate. Thomerson, though, as the administrative assistant to congressmen for over 22 years, clearly bested all the candidates in terms of his actual experience in Washington.

Commentators quickly pounced on the 5th District Democratic Party primary as one of the most interesting races in the state. Bagley got a head start on his opponents and had been campaigning in the district for weeks before the others left the starting gate. Thomerson hoped to get the support of retiring Congressman Ralph Scott, whose administrative assistant he was, but Scott said he would be neutral. However, most of the party leadership in Stokes County, Scott's home county, were now in the Bagley camp. Political observers foresaw a second primary but were generally unwilling to guess which two candidates would survive that first primary.

Eula N. Greenwood with the Waynesville *Mountaineer*, said that the race would be "a lulu." Solidly in the tobacco belt as both grower and manufacturer, the district, she said, produced half of the cigarettes and smoking tobacco sold in the United States. Bagley was viewed as the leading candidate, largely because he was handling his run in a professional way and had the money to "saturate the area with billboard, newspaper, radio, and television advertising." However, Greenwood noted that Galifianakis "has a way with him" and with sufficient exposure beyond Durham County "could be the major surprise in the race." She said Bill Wood and Nick were close friends and in a second primary the loser would support the survivor.

Jim Srodes, who had begun law study at Duke University but soon found it unfulfilling in comparison to reporting for the *Durham Herald*, became Nick's press secretary.

Despite his commitment to the candidate, Srodes saw the campaign as a preliminary skirmish that Nick could not win. However, Srodes thought the race would put Nick in a better position in a future campaign when, in all likelihood, Durham County would be joined with its neighbors in another reapportionment. In retrospect Srodes concluded that his prediction had not taken into account two matters: the contrariness of the North Carolina voter who saw the very existence of an in-group as sufficient reason to join the outsiders, and the instinctive political skill of Nick Galifianakis. Srodes once commented: "He could walk into a room full of strangers and walk away with a band of eager committed loyalists."

Nick was well-known in the capital city of Raleigh and certainly in Durham. Governor Terry Sanford, who had remembered Nick's winning campaign at Boys State in 1946, now saw Nick as "one of the bright young leaders in the state." Sanford continued: "We considered Nick a comer with a great deal to offer. He was highly intelligent and highly motivated and a person of considerable integrity." Despite such kind words from the man who controlled the state's Democratic machine, Nick was never viewed as an insider, a part of the political establishment. Although he never seemed to take offense, he did believe that divisions in the Democratic Party were harmful to its continued success in North Carolina.

By March 1966 Galifianakis was addressing national issues, especially one of increasing importance, the war in Vietnam. President Lyndon Johnson had shifted American forces from an advisory role to a fighting force. Following the Gulf of Tonkin incident, which led Congress to issue the president a blank check in terms of military action in the area, Johnson substantially increased the number of troops and made them the main force opposing North Vietnam and its sympathizers in the south. Nick's first public response to the situation was to call for winning the war as soon as possible with as many troops committed as necessary to accomplish the mission. At the same time, he suggested getting the United Nations involved in the struggle, thus substituting the troops of other member countries for some of the nation's own. Just becoming acquainted with the issue as a candidate for Congress, Nick did not realize how isolated the United States was in the struggle.

Nick on the campaign trail.

Galifianakis had formally launched his campaign on March 9, 1966, promising a new partnership between him, as their representative, and the residents of the district. He said he would "schedule regular and frequent visits to each of the communities of the district." He promised to keep in close touch with his constituents, saying that he would hold regular meetings in post offices throughout the district and, if finances permitted, maintain offices in both Durham and Winston-Salem. In April, Nick announced that Robert N. Westbrook, an engineer prominent in civic affairs, would be his campaign chairman. Along with Galifianakis, Westbrook was listed as one of the "Outstanding Young Men of America."

Nick reminded Winston-Salem voters that as a state legislator, he had been a strong supporter of both the North Carolina School for the Arts and the Governor's School, both located in that city. In a visit into this stronghold of his potential opponents, he said: "Just remember I'm that Greek fellow with the long name and the short bank account." He thus began what would become standard fare in all his campaigns, making an issue of his ethnic name and pleading poverty. Foreseeing a campaign of limited spending, he said he hoped his biggest contributions would be the modest donations of the "'little people' who encouraged him to run." He also said a person had suggested that he run the "campaign on a slogan of 'Nickels for Nick.'" Despite skeptics, Nick liked the campaign idea, and soon decorated nail kegs were placed in various places in Durham to receive nickel contributions. In fact, he sought to pay his $300 filing fee in nickels, but the three bags, each containing 2,000 nickels, were refused by Mary McCord, the State Elections Board secretary. She "did not relish the counting job or the calls from coin collectors." Nick relented and wrote a check for the $300 and became the last of the four candidates to file. The *Durham Sun* wrote in an editorial that Nick gave the 5th District contest "a new zest, a new significance, a new importance," and even "a new dignity—and a new meaning."

Stressing his legislative experience, Galifianakis announced an eight-point program that involved improving highways, expanding community college and special education programs, improving water quality and reducing air pollution, and increasing research that would strengthen the state's agriculture and key industries, such as tobacco and textiles. Nick spelled out his position on all eight issues and argued that his experience qualified him to serve in Congress. Galifianakis suggested an end to the draft, and opposition to required governmental service for young people. He opposed any increase in federal taxes and, in conformity with most North Carolinians, the housing section of a new civil rights bill that would prohibit racial discrimination in the rental or sale of housing.

The executive board of the state AFL-CIO found both Galifianakis and Wood worthy of support, but said it would endorse neither in the first of what was expected to be two primaries. Bagley's presence in the race led commentators to predict that a million dollars might be spent by the candidates, with Bagley being the big spender.

When the Democratic candidates were asked to respond to a number of questions ranging from civil rights to foreign aid, Wood refused. The answers given by Bagley and Galifianakis revealed little difference between the candidates. In an address to the Reidsville Jaycees, Nick called attention to what he referred to as "imbalances" in the federal government, spotting a problem that would only worsen over the coming years—a weak Congress unable or unwilling to challenge the other two branches of the federal government.

The four-person race, as it developed, began to look more like a two-person race: Nick Galifianakis versus Smith Bagley. It attracted the attention of Drew Pearson, whose syndicated column, *Washington Merry-Go-Round*, drew attention to the 5th District race in North Carolina. Calling them "most opposite competitors," Pearson said Bagley, the heir to the Reynolds tobacco fortune, was running up a tab of $100,000 on TV advertising to counter Nick's political experience. And Bagley turned down all invitations for a face-to-face debate. In mid-May Nick reported expenses of close to $14,000, mostly raised from contributions from Durham residents. Bagley was seen as bringing "Madison Avenue techniques to the district and establishing a middle-ground from which he could court the segregationist sentiment of the eastern part of the district while still gaining a good portion of the black vote in Forsyth County." Furthermore, the Lake Peoples Association, which had considerable support in Durham and which represented a conservative, segregationist view, threw its support to Bagley, despite opposition from some of its members. Its namesake, I. Beverly Lake, a state high court judge, had carried Durham County in his race for governor in 1964. At the same time Bagley sought to court black voters by releasing information saying he was instrumental in seeing that a Z. Smith Reynolds Foundation scholarship was awarded to a black student from Rockingham County. This attempt to court black voters apparently backfired, as Bagley's opponents accused him of using his position on the foundation for political gain.

Despite the seriousness of the competition, Nick, as usual, made time for fun and ensured his supporters had fun too. On the weekend of May 21-22, a Galifianakis caravan covered the six counties. A flat-bed truck filled with thirteen young women and Tommy Edwards' band, along with an eleven automobile entourage, barnstormed through the area from Durham to Winston-Salem. There was some confusion coming out of Walnut Grove and two cars were temporarily lost, but all was well again as the group reached a Winston-Salem shopping center. Nick also made campaigning a family affair. What he had that Smith Bagley did not, was four equally handsome and friendly brothers, three of whom filled in for the candidate when he could not be everywhere he needed to be.

The 5th Congressional district race continued to generate interest. On the eve of the first primary, *Raleigh Times* reporter William A. Shires characterized Nick as "a liberal minded public figure cut on the John F. Kennedy mold." His campaign was seen as both "aggressive and colorful." At the same time, both Wood and Thomerson had begun to criticize Bagley, not only for enticing supporters away from the other Forsyth candidates, but also for his lavish spending. Thomerson said that "the seat shouldn't be put on the block and sold to the highest bidder." Bagley had listed expenditures of $34,555.55 and had paid for almost half of the sum himself. Nick kept playing the role of the impoverished candidate, but he was second in spending to Bagley. All three opponents emphasized the facts that Bagley was young and politically inexperienced, that he had only recently become a North Carolina resident, and that he seemed to have unlimited financial resources.

When asked to respond to questions posed by the *Durham Morning Herald* addressing current issues, Nick provided the most thorough answers. Bagley chose not to respond at all, apparently conceding Durham County to his opponent. The *Winston-Salem Journal* saw Nick's entry into the race producing "some flairs of political campaign color," noting that Galifianakis had used unusual methods to draw attention to both the issues and himself. Mentioned were the "missing link" episode when he walked much of a 40-mile route that desperately needed a four lane highway and one in which he flagged down the governor's limousine, frustrated at not being able to schedule an appointment with Dan Moore regarding a proposal to increase the state tax exemption. Also noted as part of his "political showmanship" were the 6000 nickels with which Nick sought to pay the filing fee.

Color indeed is part of what Nick brought to the campaign. Galifianakis had a campaign jingle, which some people still remembered forty years later. Also, in his office in Durham he had a large clock in which the numbers had been replaced by the twelve letters of his name. In addition to the hands, the face of the clock bore the message "In the 'Nick' of time." As Lloyd Preslar said in *The Winston-Salem Journal*, "give Nick time with a stranger and he will [either] find a friend or convince the stranger that he is far too corny to be a member of Congress." The reporter added that "the former occurs far more than the latter." Nick's campaign was filled with gimmicks. When his office opened in Winston-Salem, visitors were serenaded by a disco band and offered a kiss from a pretty girl in return for a nickel contribution to the campaign. Although Preslar found the way Nick blended serious discussion of issues with the chatter about his name disconcerting, the reporter conceded that Nick was the best speaker of the four candidates. His detractors were saying that he could not win with gimmicks, but Preslar concluded that "the husky marine could be a triple threat." Therefore, despite difficulty with pronunciation, name recognition continued to grow.

Newspaper columnists also noted how Nick would spend time actually listening to people's problems, often to the annoyance of campaign staffers who had him tightly scheduled. Galifianakis gave the impression of inexhaustible energy and projected a confidence that could not be missed.

Nick had great support from both whites and blacks in Durham County, but one group, the Durham County Citizens' Council, withheld support on the basis that Nick had voted to amend the Speaker Ban Law in the last session of the North Carolina legislature. This criticism fit into a pattern that would figure in all his campaigns for national office—that the candidate was far too liberal to represent the wishes of North Carolina constituents. Certainly support for the right to work law in North Carolina, opposition to raising the minimum wage, and opposition to imposing rigid regulations on automobile manufacturers would hardly put him in the liberal camp. Galifianakis' response to the claim that he was a liberal never varied. He said he was an independent thinker who refused to be confined by labels.

While the Democrats were fighting for the nomination, who the winner would face in the general election in the fall was already decided. W. A. Nab Armfield, a retired Winston-Salem stockbroker, had been considered to be not only the likely Republican candidate, but also one who had a real chance to emerge victorious in the general election in November. This assessment was the result of his race two years earlier against the Democratic incumbent, Scott, when Armfield "came closer to winning the seat. . . than any Republican in recent history, losing by only a few thousand votes...and carrying both Forsyth and Wilkes counties." When Armfield chose not to run, G. Fred Steele, Jr., an insurance executive, became the choice of the Party. The Republican was building his organization as the Democrats were trying to decide on a nominee.

Nick continued to stress his experience as a legislator in the various forums in which the four candidates appeared. His swarthy complexion and penchant for political gimmicks offered quite a contrast with tall, WASP-y, and cultured New Yorker, Smith Bagley. The new North Carolinian tried to turn the claim that he sought to buy political office on its head, by claiming that his money should be viewed as a political asset in that a congressman who has no need of money is free to vote his convictions.

On the eve of the Democratic primary, many voters, especially in the tier of smaller counties bordering Virginia, were still undecided. Political wisdom held that the candidate that could get the most exposure immediately before the election would have an advantage with such voters. Because of his contracting for much last minute media advertising, Bagley was seen as the likely victor.

As voters went to the polls on May 28, 1966, Nick could not sit still, as he visited all of Durham County's 38 precincts. Whoever emerged victorious would in all likelihood have to endure a second primary. The *Greensboro News* did offer the opinion that, if the substantial black populations of Durham and Forsyth were to cast their votes for one of the candidates, it could be the decisive factor.

Conforming to expectations, Nick did extremely well in Durham County where he won by over a six to one count and he carried Rockingham County, thus overcoming larger votes for Bagley in the other four counties. His total margin of victory over Bagley was slightly less than 4,000 votes. The celebration at Durham headquarters started early, and Nick's mother, Sophie, and his wife, Louise, joined the brothers, including teen-aged John but not Mike, who was representing Nick at the Winston-Salem office. Nick had 37% of the votes, Bagley 31% and the other two candidates a combined 32%. Thomerson, who ran last, must have been quite disappointed in that the citizens of the district in which he had served as the congressman's assistant had not returned the favor. Wood, who was expected to pick up the black vote in Forsyth and then in a second primary have Nick fall heir to those votes was disappointed when Bagley, despite segregationist support, gained the majority of those votes. Yet, as expected, Nick would pick up many former Wood supporters in the inevitable second Democratic primary.

Galifianakis had come out at the head of the primary field, but he now faced a second election, and if Bagley could capture the majority of votes cast for Wood and Thomerson, the other two Forsyth County candidates, the man from Durham would be defeated.

98

INTERLUDE 6

Campaigning as Entertainment

In the end, Nick Galifianakis' opponent in his first race for Congress, Smith Bagley, could not escape his elitist background or his wealth. With money beginning to play a significant role in politics in the 1960s, an observer might ask how it became a liability in Bagley's campaign. Somehow, throughout the campaign, Bagley was put on the defensive, having to argue that rich people could serve the public as well as those with more limited resources. It confused him. Did not money afford the individual a freedom of action denied to those who inevitably had to depend on the contributions of others? Regularly pleading poverty and noting his social status as a regular joe, Galifianakis had hit a much more responsive chord.

With no great policy differences separating the men, Bagley relied upon his sophistication and good looks to appeal to voters, while Galifianakis took a common "nice guy, I'm really one of you" or "hail fellow well met" approach. A detractor might well conclude that Nick, with two degrees from a prestigious university and a reputation for being a very effective lawyer, was hiding who he was behind a political façade. But those who knew him said there was no difference between Galifianakis the campaigner and Galifianakis the man. And the voters must have sensed that. For Bagley, politics was a serious business that was demeaned by the crude appeals of a showman; he would not, and in fact, could not "descend" to that level. Nick, on the other hand, believed that voters responded to a "bread and circuses" approach. In fact, history confirmed his belief that political gatherings were a form of entertainment. Indeed, long before the advent of entertainment challenges from radio, motion pictures and television, politics was almost all there was.

Bagley sought to dismiss Galifianakis' antics as "publicity stunts." At a barbecue dinner for supporters, he said that his opponent was staging a "carnival sideshow." Bagley hoped that 5th District voters would not be "taken in by a flimflam campaign . . ., go-go girls and penny candy." (The penny candy was a reference to the hard candy that Nick attached to his brochures. While handing them out he would refer to the candy saying that they were "pep pills" or that he wanted to leave "a sweet impression.") Bagley concluded by suggesting that citizens should select the candidate who was seeking their support in a dignified and honest way rather than one who was "trying to hoodwink or bamboozle with empty talk and silly gimmicks." One cannot but sympathize with a well-intentioned candidate who was being outmaneuvered, as Bagley was.

Others, once they realized they were beaten, just got on the bandwagon. It reflects on Galifianakis' essential likeability that both Smith and his wife Vicki became Nick's friends. In fact, in one of Nick's subsequent campaigns Vicki was able to convince one of the Reynolds' heirs to make a substantial donation.

Nick with the sheriff of Rockingham County on the campaign trail.

His entertaining style stayed with Nick into his Senate campaign. He is here with Senator Sam Ervin, Jr. (Note the young women in the background!)

CHAPTER VII

The Second Primary and General Election, 1966

Well short of a majority, Galifianakis would face Bagley in a second primary. Having come in last in Forsyth County, Nick knew any road to success had to run through that county's largest city, Winston-Salem. For that to happen, he had to win the favor of the Thomerson and Wood supporters. As he contemplated the race, Nick decided that he would characterize the main issue in the campaign as experience versus inexperience. He stressed the fact that as a member of the North Carolina House, he had proposed and steered legislation through the General Assembly that helped people in all the counties of the district.

The second primary was scheduled for June 25. Nick tried to engage Bagley in a series of debates, but Bagley again refused. The first primary left some hard feelings on the part of losing candidates Wood and Thomerson regarding the way in which Bagley conducted his campaign. Although there was a call for Forsyth to unify as Durham did behind the resident candidate, and some concern that Durham might not be in the 5th District in the coming reapportionment, the bitter taste left from the first election undermined the effort. Galifianakis was therefore able to line up the support of all of Wood's county campaign managers and four of Thomerson's. Bagley, on the other hand, received the endorsement of the retiring 5th District Congressman, Ralph J. Scott. Scott's wife, however, jumped on Nick's bandwagon, as did Thomerson's wife.

Bagley and his supporters not only continued to criticize

Nick's campaign gimmicks but they also sought to escape the charge that Bagley was the candidate of wealth. The former mayor of Winston-Salem, a Bagley supporter, called attention to the fact that Galifianakis received contributions from a number of millionaires in Durham, who just might want something for their investment. On the other hand, Bagley added, he was using his own money, implying that he wouldn't be beholden to anyone.

Building on the success of the flatbed truck with dancing girls, Nick decided to offer a free night of baseball to Forsyth County residents. For $1.000, he rented the Ernie Shore Field for "Nick Galifianakis for Congress Night" on June 16. With the help of the Forsyth Committee for Good Government, a pro-Galifianakis group, he treated over 5,000 fans, a 500% increase in normal attendance, to a game between the Winston-Salem Red Sox and the Portsmouth Tides. He had used baseball analogies in his campaign earlier, but now he was using an actual game. Before the game, the candidate took the mound. After some wildness with his first five pitches, Nick sent his next three pitches over the plate and retired to the Red Sox dugout. Taking advantage of this unusual setting, Nick promised no long speeches, but he did draw a baseball analogy: "I have trained myself and conditioned myself in the minor leagues of politics. Now I want to go to the majors. I want to be your congressman." He then introduced his family, including his daughter, 3-year old Katherine, and his brothers Harry, Mike and Pete.

The game ball was to be delivered by sky divers whose goal was to land near a smoke flair set off at second base, but high altitude winds had blown the three skydivers off-course. They had to walk to the stadium to deliver the game ball. If the skydivers' part of the extravaganza did not work out quite as dramatically as intended, the weather, which provided a scare, eventually did. Early rain came down in torrents, but an hour before the game the sky cleared. The general manager of the Red Sox was accused of selling the game to Nick, and rumors surfaced that he had been pressured by Bagley supporters to cancel the arrangement. His response was that any legitimate group had the same opportunity that had been granted to Nick's campaign.

This latest episode was just too much for Smith Bagley, who had already been accused of seeking to buy his way into office and of thwarting the democratic process by refusing to debate Nick. One can imagine how frustrated a candidate with Bagley's connections and background could get in trying to contend with Nick's flamboyant style of campaigning and grass-roots appeal.

Attacking Nick's electioneering gimmicks did not provide much traction, so Bagley also criticized Nick's record in the North Carolina legislature. This strategy was a calculated gamble, calling attention to the fact that Galifianakis had the legislative experience that the transplanted New Yorker did not. At any rate, Nick, responding to the charges, said that his record clearly showed he supported popular initiatives such as pay raises for teachers in the 1965 session, pushed for tax relief, and consistently supported the tobacco industry.

Bagley also resented a number of recent cartoons that played upon his wealth in a clever way. The cartoon in the *Durham Morning Herald* accompanied a column that talked of Bagley trying to buy his seat in Congress, which concluded that the coming vote "would determine whether it is easier for a Camel to go through the eye of a needle than for a rich man to go to Heaven." The cartoon depicted Bagley with a cigarette in one hand and a needle in the other with the Capitol labeled Heaven. The cigarette is ragged, apparently from repeated attempts to pass it through the needle. Nearby is Galifianakis with a "Pick Nick" sign, saying "I don't think you can."

The *Greensboro Daily News* cartoon showed Bagley on a camel whose hide is filled with dollar signs being passed by Nick who has raised a cloud of dust, with Bagley saying "Follow that car." (Apparently Bagley felt that the latter cartoon was less insulting, for he accepted a gift of the original from the cartoonist.)

As explained, the old 5th District did not include Durham County; instead it included Surry and Granville Counties. Bagley tried to get some mileage out of this change, saying that he would work to put the old district back together when the North Carolina legislature responded to a court order in the 1967 session. Nick realized that if the run-off primary was to be viewed by voters as a contest between Durham and Forsyth Counties, he would in all likelihood lose because of Forsyth's greater population. Therefore, he skirted the possibility that Forsyth might be placed in another district in a subsequent reapportionment.

As late as June 16, 1966 – nine days before the second primary - Thomerson refused to throw his support to either candidate, but a week later he joined his wife's support of Nick and made a public statement to that effect. The common assumption was that despite no public announcement, Wood, the third highest vote-getter in the first primary, who was a friend of Nick's and had served with him in the North Carolina legislature, was an implicit supporter. Though he would not make a formal endorsement, Wood did tell former aides that he would vote for Nick. What these actions did was deprive Bagley of at least some of the votes of his two Forsyth County opponents, which together had added up to as many votes as he received in the first primary. Although all those disappointed voters would not necessarily

The cartoon.

follow their candidate's lead, the solid Forsyth front was splintered. The reason for the estrangement between Wood and Thomerson and Bagley resulted from some personality differences but was also the result of a feeling that Bagley's heavily financed campaign undercut the other Forsyth County candidates.

Nick spent 75% of the time since the first primary in Winston-Salem and Forsyth County, and Bagley spent considerable time in Durham. 60, 747 people voted in the first primary; election officials forecasted a drop of less than 20% in the election scheduled for June 25th. Weekly newspapers were split on the candidates. The *Kernersville News* in Forsyth County and The *Danbury Reporter* in Stokes County endorsed Bagley. The *Madison Messenger* in Rockingham and the *King Times-News* in Stokes supported Galifianakis.

At a meeting of the Winston-Salem Board of Realtors, the candidates, including Republican Fred Steele, were offered a chance to speak. Bagley begged off, citing other commitments, but his place was taken by a supporter who attacked Galifianakis, accusing him of buying black votes in Durham and saying that he would be "a rubber stamp for the administration in Washington now." Steele took a similar approach by attacking Lyndon Johnson's Great Society programs. Nick was still discussing issues as election day approached. He suggested the draft be eliminated and reserve units relied upon to strengthen forces when needed. He was interested in seeking a settlement in Vietnam, and pointed to a special need for the Congress of the United States to maintain the checks and balances the Constitution intended. After all, it was the people's "working branch." One editorial put the choice before the voters as "whether you prefer a big spender or a fast talker." On the eve of the primary Drew Pearson in a second column said Bagley was trying to buy himself the seat in Congress and that Thomerson had been offered a new house if he would drop out of the race before the first primary. Bagley called the accusation a lie. The conclusion, even in 1966, was that being a big spender gave one an edge. As the campaign was ending, Nick reported that his campaign had cost $18, 565 and contributions had come up short by about $1900. Bagley reported expenses of almost $52,000.

The 5th District race had attracted special interest, but when the number of voters in the second primary eclipsed the first by 1,111 everyone was surprised. Nick's margin of victory exceeded 4,000 votes, the count being 32,967 to 28, 891. Galifianakis now won Rockingham County, meaning the two candidates split the counties in the district. The difference was Nick's much more substantial showing in Forsyth County. Although Bagley garnered almost 16,000 votes there, Galifianakis had over 9,000, a much greater inroad than Bagley had been able to make in Durham County, where Nick had an 11,600 vote advantage.

The votes had been tallied quickly, and Bagley conceded before 8 p.m. Overjoyed, Nick thanked the Forsyth voters who, he said, were key to his electoral victory. In Winston-Salem Bagley pledged his support, as did Bill Wood, who Nick called the "fellow without whom this couldn't have happened." Had the other two Winston-Salem candidates, Thomerson and Wood endorsed Bagley, thus providing a united Forsyth County front, Nick probably would have lost the second primary. Although Wood never formally endorsed Nick, his widespread organization had joined Nick's campaign. Now he responded to the accolades given to Galifianakis by offering one of his own. Winston-Salem, Wood said, clearly deserved the "All American City" designation by casting 9100 votes for the son of Greek immigrants, who he now claimed would be the best representative sent to Congress by any North Carolina district.

Although Bagley confessed that he did not know whether the Drew Pearson columns had hurt or helped his campaign, he did pay Pearson a visit to argue that wealth should not be a bar to political service. Bagley noted that it was not only Pearson but several North Carolina newspapers that had argued that North Carolinians should register their belief that one from a humble origin had equal opportunity to serve the nation. He protested that men of wealth should not be denied their opportunity to contribute to the public good. Pearson called Bagley a "good loser" and agreed, but then said that there simply were not enough wealthy candidates to fill the offices of government.

Mama Sophie congratulates Nick on his victory in the primary.

One newspaper had called the 5th District contest "undoubtedly the hottest congressional primary here in 20 years." Commending Bagley's "impressive showing, it said that North Carolina newspapers viewed him . . . as a potential congressman two years from now if Durham is placed in another district." The paper had correctly predicted that Durham would be severed from the 5th District and that Bagley would become the Democratic candidate for another congressional seat in 1968. Bagley's last attempt to win a congressional seat, however, was embarrassingly squashed when he lost to a Republican. That Republican was Wilmer Mizell, a pitcher who had played in the major leagues for over a decade, mainly with the St. Louis Cardinals and Pittsburgh Pirates. Bagley probably never understood why he had been bested both by a showman and by a baseball player.

Galifianakis quickly turned from the euphoria of victory in June to preparing for the campaign against Republican Fred Steele. When there were general election contests, which had not always been the case in the Democratic South, the survivor of the Democratic primaries tended to win easily. But Nick took nothing in politics for granted. Clearly their positions were well staked out. When Steele opened his Durham campaign office, he reiterated the Republican mantra: his opponent would have to defend the Democratic administration's "reckless spending policies, its excessive and endless grasping for more power for the federal government, and its conduct of U. S. foreign policy, including the war in Vietnam." Steele saw victory ahead as he put his opponent in the position of defending what the Republican considered largely indefensible policies.

Nick did have to put his continuous campaigning on hold during two weeks of the summer when he was called up for a training tour with the Marine reserves in which he had risen to the rank of major. He spent part of the time escorting two Korean officers, who had difficulty in saying his last name. He indicated to them that this problem was not new, and, in fact, as he dealt with other foreigners, he found that the pronunciation "adjusted to fit just about any nationality."

Galifianakis said the major issues confronting the nation were the Vietnam war and inflation. In regard to the war, he saw encouraging signs that could lead to peace, and he felt that some inflation could be attributed to the nation's prosperity. He acknowledged that his party may have made mistakes, but he said he found few constructive suggestions for solutions to any problems from the Republicans. They "not only want to stand still", he said, "they often want to go backwards."

The general election campaign ran a poor second to the primary campaigns. Steele sought to take advantage of a growing disillusionment with the Johnson presidency on the part of North Carolina voters. Lyndon B. Johnson, the Texan in the White House with a substantial Democratic majority in the Congress, embraced both the civil rights crusade and the Great Society. These positions left considerable room for a revived Republican Party to capitalize on Southern resentment and become a viable political option in a region, which had, for so long, found little attraction in Abraham Lincoln's party. But Johnson was not running, and Nick was able to carve out his own political niche and rely upon his vigorous campaigning and prior political experience to carry him to victory. His expenditure of $14,690 was considerably less than what he had spent defeating Bagley in the primaries.

In the general election on November 8, 1966, Galifianakis outpolled Steele by a 46,035 to 40,729 count and became the 5th District's new congressman. After the public celebration of the victory, Nick invited a young *Durham Morning Herald* reporter, Bob Page to join the family in a private celebration involving an assortment of Greek foods prepared by Nick's mother, Miss Sophie. Galifianakis praised the reporter for his balanced coverage of the campaign. Shortly thereafter, Nick put his head down between his arms and began crying. The reporter was perplexed; Nick had won, not lost. When the new congressman could speak, he said he was sad that his father was not here to see his eldest son elected to Congress. Galifianakis then proceeded to explain the debt that he owed to his parents who had sacrificed so much to provide for their sons. Then Nick told again of his father's good nature and unabashed patriotism. Page long remembered that special occasion, and he never could talk about it without again getting choked up, as he did on the night of Nick's first election to Congress.

Nick and his wife, Louise, after his first Congressional victory.

Change was in the air. Many reporters credited the black vote for being the deciding factor in the race. The Southern Regional Council agreed, and added that twenty blacks were elected to Southern legislatures, an increase of nine. Political observers cautioned that the overall results in the state, including Nick's race, showed new Republican Party strength. Nick had lost Forsyth County by 3,000 votes, not a bad showing given the county's growing Republican character. Reporters suggested that the loser, Steele, might try again in 1968. Having Galifianakis' record in the House to criticize, the Republican might be able to reverse the result of 1966.

Nick could now concentrate his attention on becoming an active member of Congress. On a trip to Washington, he was surprised to find so many people there knowledgeable about the district and his electoral victory. On a trip to Winston-Salem in December, he outlined his present intentions to a *Journal* reporter. Recognizing that his freshman status limited his options, he said he hoped to be appointed to a seat on the House Appropriations Committee, which was, along with the Rules and Ways and Means Committee, among the most influential committees. He had no specific legislation to introduce, but said he would not hesitate to do so if something came up. He added that as a new congressman, it was more realistic to look forward to co-sponsoring bills.

Celebrating victory with his mother, Sophia.

Realism aside, Galifianakis, would not be content play-ing the role of a silent freshman member of Congress.

INTERLUDE 7

Nick's Celebrated Sense of Humor

Nick had a well-cultivated sense of humor coupled with a heartfelt laugh that was easily triggered when others said something funny. Others may see politics as a serious business, but Galifianakis maintained that "spirit of levity is important to legislative sanity."

Nick's penchant for humor was revealed early in his Nickelodian columns for the *Hi-Rocket*, Durham High School's newspaper. In addition to the puns and poems, the columns were filled with wordplay, such as: "Spring is here at last! The sap runneth, but the girl catcheth him anyhow." In question and answer form, the column contained bits such as the following:

Q: Name two ancient sports.

A: Anthony and Cleopatra.

Q: Can you say how long girls should be loved?

A: The same as short girls.

The wordplay that entertained Durham High School students remained a part of Nick's sense of humor. At times, though, his wordplay incurred groans rather than smiles. For instance, when at a White House dinner in honor of the Ethiopian emperor, Haile Selassie, Galifianakis remarked to his dinner companion that if the emperor had a sister, her name might well be "Silly Assi." A more successful attempt he brought to bear at a Federation of Hellenic Societies banquet in New York City on March 26, 1972, noting that the organization was composed of 95 different groups with a total of approximately 30,000 members. After saying his fellow North Carolinians would be impressed with his moving in such high society, he added: "Please understand that my use of the term 'high' pertains to numbers only, and not the chemical content of our collective bloodstreams."

At times in his Nickelodian columns, Galifianakis went beyond word play, like when he defined a politician as "a guy who contrasts his wings and halo against his opponent's horns and tail." Or when he said there was a campaign to change the color of the uniform postal workers wore, because "Every time a Northerner sees one of those grey uniforms his trigger finger itches."

Another element of his sense of humor involved making fun of undue formality or seriousness, pretentiousness or pomposity, something that began when he was a youngster. We can see it when he took on Smith Bagley in his race for Congress by being the clown, or when he deliberately assumed the role of the less sophisticated Southerner that often led others to underestimate his intelligence and political savvy.

When this trait was expressed verbally, it dovetailed into the third element of his sense of humor: self-deprecation. This was his favored approach. Examples of this element are found usually at the beginning of his many speeches, a usually successful attempt to win the favor of the audience. One of the oft repeated stories he told on himself that went over extremely well with audiences was the following:

Really, that was a heart-warming introduction. You should have heard the one I had recently down in North Carolina. The lady who was supposed to introduce me was having a terrible time pronouncing Galifianakis. She tried and tried before giving up, simply saying "And now we'll hear the latest dope from Washington."

Looking back on it, I think that lady may have been try-ing to tell me something. After the speech, she came up to me and said: "Your remarks were simply super-fluous!" I didn't know whether she was kidding or not, but I decided to play along with her. I thanked her kindly and told her that I was thinking of having the speech published posthumously. She replied: "The sooner the better."

Perhaps precisely because of this aspect of his speech-making, Nick was much in demand. He was a favorite speaker at gatherings of Greek-Americans. But he also spoke at gatherings that involved civic organizations and political groups, honored holidays and veterans, energized conferences and dedications, and enlivened commence-ments.

As the commencement speaker at Cary High School, Nick began by quoting Adlai Stevenson, the Democratic candidate for president in 1952 and 1956, when Stevenson addressed a Princeton University graduating class:

I've been at a loss what to say to you, and having just read over what I prepared rather hastily, I have conclud-ed that I have resolved my uncertainty by saying noth-ing. This will take me approximately 40 minutes.

Saying then that since he "would be flattered to be half as articulate and half as eloquent" as Stevenson, Nick said he would "only speak for approximately 20 minutes." As for giving advice to the graduates, Galifianakis said he was reluctant, being reminded of a youngster who was asked to explain who Socrates was. The boy responded: "Socrates was a wise man. He went around giving advice. They poi-soned him."

John E. Semonche

120

CHAPTER VIII

Welcome to Congress, 1967

On January 10, 1967 Nick Galifianakis took the oath of office as the representative of North Carolina's 5th Congressional District. The *Durham Morning Herald* paid tribute to the new representative. It said "he was born in the expansive old Imperial Fifth which included, in addition to the district's present counties, all the counties in the old Sixth in which he grew to manhood and embarked on his political career." Summing up his record of prior political service, the editorialist said of Nick "the new Fifth stands assured of representation by a hard-working congressman who keeps abreast of the issues, keeps in close touch with the voters and, as an independent thinker, acts at all times in what he considers the best interest of the district and the nation."

On the eve of Nick's being sworn in as a member of the 90th Congress, the *Durham Morning Herald* also ran a story covering the entire first page of the Sunday features section with the headline: "Mr. G. Goes to Washington." The obvious allusion to Frank Capra's film, *Mr. Smith Goes to Washington*, with Jimmy Stewart in the title role, seemed especially apt. First of all, both Mr. Smith and Mr. G. were unlikely selections, for Smith had no political experience and Galifianakis had a foreign name, limited financial resources, and only tenuous political establishment support. Like Smith, Galifianakis was a combination of political naiveté and sophistication, intent upon making his voice heard on behalf of the people, many of whom had placed their trust in him. The difference was that Mr. Smith had not earned his seat, while Mr. Galifianakis certainly had. Smith had been chosen by party bosses who believed that they could easily manipulate him, while Galifianakis was chosen by himself and had to survive some tough elections.

Freshman Congressman Galifianakis.

Charles Barbour, the reporter who wrote the story and who accompanied Nick to Raleigh to clean out his office there in preparation for his new role in Washington, could not get to the questions he originally wanted to ask. Nick's excitement over his new responsibilities bubbled over and captured the reporter. Barbour was impressed by his subject's active role in the North Carolina legislature and wondered whether he could quickly become a leader in the nation's House of Representatives. Nick said he wanted his constituents to know that they had a voice in Washington, but that he would not presume to know answers when he was only learning the questions. He said he wanted his constituents to view him as a member of their families or simply as the boy next door. "I hope," he said, "to make a spirit of service my polar star." What he would do, he said, was get to know those persons who shaped legislation, and study the rules, procedures, customs and traditions of the House, hopefully impressing the power structure with his willingness to learn and work hard. This approach was ingrained in Nick. Both as a lawyer and legislator, he realized the value of knowledge.

As a congressman, Nick's salary was $30,000, and it would be raised to $42,000 in 1969. That amount was substantially supplemented by allowances for staff, office space, travel, and other expenses. To earn that salary and fulfill his mission of service, Nick realized that he needed some guidance in dealing with his responsibilities in the nation's capital, so he worked to create a top-notch staff. First, he readily agreed to employ his former opponent in the Democratic primary, Harold Thomerson, as his administrative assistant. Thomerson had sought the job because he needed six more months of government service to increase his retirement pay. Thomerson had not only served in that capacity for the now retired Ralph Scott, but he had served Scott's predecessors going back to 1944. After six months, Thomerson left and his position was filled internally by Margaret Sugg, who would remain the anchor of the office as long as Nick was in Congress. Fifteen other individuals comprised the staff, one more than the norm because Nick's district was so extensive.

Barbara Fletcher, the assistant director, was a key staff member and hired shortly after Nick took office. (Her politics were the polar opposite of those of her grandfather, A. J. Fletcher, who owned both the radio and television station WRAL in Raleigh. His politics were right wing, expressed over the airwaves by Jesse Helms. Helms' favorite targets were the federal government, the civil rights movement and the print press.) Galifianakis put his campaign press secretary Jim Srodes on his legislative payroll. Joan Goren of Durham, and Lucy Ann Weir from Winston-Salem also joined the Galifianakis camp. Weir had been the secretary of the Democratic Party in Forsyth County, and now Nick hired her to staff a congressional office in Winston-Salem on a full-time basis. He was the first North Carolina congressman to maintain a full-time staffed office in the district he represented. He decided to do so because he believed that not all his constituents would be able to funnel their requests through his Washington office. Also, with the Winston-Salem office he would be better able to keep in touch with his constituents and their needs. He completed the key components of his Washington staff when he added Gloria Gold, who had worked for Harold Cooley in the 4th District, and Robin Horn on a part-time basis. In time, the office would be decorated with a rotating selection of the work of North Carolina artists.

Galifianakis' staff would change over time. Among the changes was his hiring of Eric Michaux, a recent law school graduate and member of a politically prominent African-American Durham family. Nick believed that he was the first Southern congressman to hire a black staffer. Charles W. Rangel, a black New York congressman, noted the racial integration of Nick's staff. In turn, Galifianakis noted that Rangel's staff was all-white.

Nick's office, suite 1729 in the Longworth Building, was usually opened by Jim Srodes at 7 a.m. and would generally be open for twelve or more hours. Galifianakis' presence there was erratic, following no set schedule. Nick, however, insisted that visitors be treated with respect and their requests properly handled whether he was in the office or out. In addition, as he had done on the campaign trail and would continue to do, he eagerly welcomed students. He not only enjoyed their company but also shared his enthusiasm for politics with them.

Nick was one of two new faces in the North Carolina delegation. The other was Jim Gardner, the Republican from the 4th District, who had defeated Harold Cooley, the incumbent Democrat. Seated in the first row with other newcomers, Nick discreetly waived to relatives in the gallery including his mother. In a little over thirty-eight years, Mama Sophie had moved from the Capitol rotunda to the House gallery—her baby had become a congressman. No wonder she beamed. When his name was called by the clerk of the House of Representatives, Sophie Galifianakis applauded. Her son whispered "thank you." After the swearing in, Nick hosted an open house in the Longworth Building where, to no one's surprise, Mama Sophie's Greek pastries were served.

Washington in the late 1960s was an especially exciting place, and the congressional hopper was filled with bills President Lyndon Johnson was pushing as part of his Great Society program. With the American military presence in Vietnam growing, Johnson assured the nation that it could have both guns and butter, meaning, that he believed war spending could be accommodated without sacrificing the creation of the Great Society.

The first vote Nick cast was on the question of whether to exclude Adam Clayton Powell from the seat to which he had been elected by his Harlem district in New York City. He had been accused of diverting House committee funds to personal uses, among other allegations of corruption. Galifianakis had had an interesting exchange with Powell who wondered how a person with such a mouthful of a name could ever be elected from a Southern state. In a self-deprecating way Nick responded that he wondered about that also.

Not only the foreign-sounding name but the politics of the new representative seemed out-of-kilter. Although Nick decried labels and thought of himself as an independent thinker, others called him a liberal. On balance, he seemed to come closer to that side of the political spectrum, which often would put him at odds with others in the North Carolina delegation. Actually, he found the members of the Massachusetts delegation, including House Speaker John M. McCormack, more politically congenial than his colleagues from the Old North State.

Nick had been asked by the North Carolina delegation to provide a memorandum addressing the issue of the House's authority to exclude Powell. Galifianakis complied. He concluded that the House had no authority to refuse to seat a member who met the constitutional qualifications of having reached the age of 25 and having been duly elected by his district. Any wrongdoing would have to be dealt with after the person was seated, when House rules could then address the matter. Nick's conclusion was rejected by the others who believed that the constitutional requirements did not prevent the House from providing additions to them. Not inclined as a new member to argue for his conclusion against the experienced members of the delegation,

Nick joined the others in voting to exclude Powell, making the vote unanimous. Powell sought to characterize his opponents as racists, but Galifianakis said that such a charge was only "a masquerade for the true facts involved." The final vote was 364 to 64. What makes Nick's memorandum especially interesting is that it anticipated the rationale that the United States Supreme Court would use in reversing the House decision and upholding Powell's right to be seated.

In addition to the Powell vote, Nick was led by the North Carolina delegation to successfully attack the 21-day rule. In the previous Congress Democratic liberals had succeeded in establishing a regulation that imposed upon the powerful House Rules Committee, which was the gateway through which proposed legislation made its way to the floor for a vote, a time limit for its consideration. Within 21 days, the Committee would be required to submit measures that had been approved by the appropriate committee to the entire House. The purpose, of course, was to reduce the power of the House Rules Committee. Republicans and Southern Democrats had voted against instituting the rule and now took the opportunity with the new Congress to repeal it.

Nick's first day in Congress taxed the young man, for the House was in session from noon to 7 p.m. Galifianakis also had to balance his new legislative responsibilities with receptions and social gatherings. To attend the celebrations in the Longworth Building he had to dash across Pennsylvania Avenue to greet well-wishers, including both Tarheel senators, B. Everett Jordan and Sam Ervin, Jr., and some fellow congressmen. He returned to Congress for the joint session that heard President Johnson's State of the Union address. The next morning Nick met with the Speaker of the House, John McCormack, until noon when the House session began.

One four-term Democratic congressman was especially pleased to welcome Nick, seeing in this new representative from a Southern state a promising recruit. The congressman was Morris K. (Mo) Udall who introduced himself as a one-eyed Mormon from Arizona. Since his first election in 1960 at the age of 38 he sought reform in the way in which the House conducted its business. He was especially unhappy with the seniority system that placed so much power in committee chairmen, saying that obtaining such a position increased the holder's power in the body by 1000 percent. Udall had found other young colleagues attracted to reforming the seniority system. Now he saw the possibility that he could include Nick in his quest for reform, making an inroad in the solid Democratic South with its vested interest in the present system.

What gave Udall special appeal to freshmen was not only his youth, engaging personality and self-deprecating humor but also his co-authorship of a book entitled *The Job of the Congressman*. The book was primarily designed to acquaint new members with both how the body operated and the range of their new responsibilities. In fact, he held an orientation session for the new arrivals which Galifianakis attended. Especially appreciating each other's sense of humor, the men became friends. Nick devoured the primer that Udall had published and quickly felt comfortable within the legislative chamber.

However, Udall's hope that he could enlist Nick in his fight against the establishment was dashed two years later when the Arizonian challenged the system by running against the incumbent for the Speaker's position at the start of the 91st Congress in early 1969. Udall counted on members such as Nick, but when the numbers were counted the incumbent, John W. McCormack of Massachusetts easily won. Mo realized that he was not going to win and therefore released the young Southerner from any obligation their friendship might have imposed. Udall realized that Nick could not desert his delegation in its support for McCormack. The Speaker had consistently supported North Carolina's major economic interests in tobacco and textiles. Furthermore, the moderation that would characterize Galifianakis' entire political career placed limits on what, in the final analysis, he could support. While Udall completely rejected the "go along to get along" approach, Nick at times embraced it. Such differences, however, did not compromise their friendship. At a meeting at which Udall was the principal speaker, Nick's introduction included the following: "He has been my guide, my teacher, and my very good friend."

In Washington, Nick quickly became a part of the capital's social scene. Among the early events was a luncheon at the Greek Embassy in honor of Princess Irene of Greece. Nick had met the princess earlier during her three-day tour of North Carolina. Galifianakis was also a guest at the White House for a dinner in honor of King Haile Selassie of Ethiopia. After dinner, guests were serenaded by opera stars Richard Tucker and Nedda Casei. Nick said he "had a good time . . . met some nice folks and had some interesting conversations." Among the other guests were Benny Goodman, the jazz musician, a couple of astronauts, civil rights leader A. Philip Randolph, and columnist Drew Pearson. Nick's wife Louise did not attend the dinner. She was pregnant and back in Durham, but she had been at the White House the previous week at a party for new congressmen and their wives.

The first bill Nick introduced in the House came at the behest of North Carolina Senator Sam Ervin, Jr. who had asked Galifianakis to introduce legislation seeking to protect the constitutional rights of federal governmental employees and prohibit the invasion of their privacy. Nick indicated both his pride in being asked to introduce the measure and his support of its purposes. The legislation eventually became law in 1974.

The dinner duties of a congressman and his wife. Here with Postmaster General Larry O'Brien.

In February, Nick was asked for his recommendation for a postmaster to fill a vacancy in his district. The request led him to question the process of filling such governmental positions. He believed that such positions should be filled under rules of the civil service and not be a matter of political patronage. Galifianakis did not want to leave the wrong impression, saying that he certainly had no objection to such appointments when the appointee came under the appointer's direct control. Here, he said, a congressman has no control of local postal officials and generally does not know who are the best qualified candidates. On the other hand, his fellow congressmen were quite happy to keep within their control federal jobs that they could confer to their political advantage. The *Greensboro Daily News* commended Nick's willingness to question the patronage scheme.

Nick Galifianakis was not the first Greek-American to be elected to Congress. He was preceded eight years earlier by John Brademas from Indiana, who had a Greek father and an American mother. Also elected in 1966 was another congressman of Greek descent, Peter N. Kyros from Maine. Nick, however, was the first Greek-American congressman who was born to both a mother and father who were born in Greece and came to the United States as young adults.

In his first month in Congress Galifianakis and the other two congressmen of Greek descent had joined Vice-President Hubert Humphrey for a flight to Chicago to attend a celebration honoring the head of the Greek Orthodox Church in the Americas, Archbishop Iakovos, born Demetrios Koukouzis. Brademas told the vice-president that the three congressmen demonstrated "an example of Greek power."

Perhaps because he embraced his heritage, combined with the Greek Orthodox faith, Galifianakis became a center of attention for the Greek community in the United States. Nick often referred to himself as Cretan, a reference to the island of Crete where both his mother and father had been born. Galifianakis was so constantly in demand both for spiritual as well as secular gatherings involving Greeks that he feared that it would interfere with his legislative tasks. Nick had at times told his administrative assistant to put a hold on "Greek things." However, he did not spurn the contributions and support he received from prominent Greeks. Perhaps no single individual was more important to Nick than Kostas Maliotis, president of the American Pan Cretan Association of America.

Galifianakis never hesitated to tell all those who would listen that the Greeks invented democracy and that their influence was readily visible in Washington. When he toured the Capitol with freshmen congressmen, Nick told them that the columns on the Capitol were Corinthian and those on the Supreme Court building Doric, both borrowings from the Greeks. When they came to the fresco on the Capitol's dome, Galifianakis said that the artist who painted the scenes, Constantino Brumidi was really Greek, though the Italians also claimed him. (Nick would concede that both countries had legitimate claims, for the artist's father was Greek and his mother was Italian.) Galifianakis also joined in sponsoring a House resolution commemorating the 200th anniversary of the first known landing of Greeks in the New World.

In an address in Boston in May, 1967 on the anniversary of Greek independence, Galifianakis pointed to the birth in ancient Greece of moderation and law, harmony and justice, and freedom and liberty. He then added words that captured his personal faith: "Our church, which forms the center of every Hellenic community, is a strong spiritual force among Americans of all faiths." Galifianakis did not parade his religion publicly, believing in the separation of church and state, but his faith was an important component of his being and a spur to his attempts to be of service to others. At times at such gatherings Nick was assumed to have been born in Greece. He quickly corrected those who so believed when that assumption came to his attention. Despite his embrace of his Greek heritage, Galifianakis was proud of his American nationality.

Nick's pride in identifying Greece with democracy took a battering when a military coup occurred on April 21, 1967. The Regime of the Colonels brought the trappings of dictatorship to the country. An attempt of the young King Constantine to stage a countercoup in December failed and the junta would control Greece until July 24, 1974. The king, in exile in Rome, would remain Head of State until the military government abolished the monarchy in 1973. Galifianakis, to his surprise, was asked by Senator Everett Dirksen to join some senators in a meeting designed to determine what position the United States should take in regard to the military junta now in control of Greece. The question posed to the group was just how much pressure should the United States place on the military government to move it toward the restoration of constitutional rule. The colonels had taken control by playing upon the fear of a communist takeover in the upcoming elections. That concern was shared by American policy makers, who remembered that the Truman Doctrine had saved Greece from a communist takeover following World War II.

One of the most outspoken critics of the military regime was the actress Melina Mercouri, who had gained visibility in the United States with her 1960 movie *Never on Sunday*, the story of a carefree prostitute who never worked on the Sabbath. When Nick came to Congress, Mercouri was preparing to star in a Broadway musical, *Illya Darling*, based upon that movie. Informed that Nick Galifianakis would be debuting about the same time in Washington, she said she was indeed proud of him and wished him all the best.

Ten days after the opening of the musical on Broadway, the junta took control in Greece. Mercouri then balanced her Broadway commitment with lobbying activity to get the United States to condemn the establishment of military government in her country. She became frustrated, as Cold War worries about communism in the United States trumped concerns for protecting democracy, leading the administration to recognize the new government and to continue military aid.

On a trip to Washington in October, 1967, her emotions boiled over when she confronted Nick in the House of Representatives dining room. Shouting, she berated him for not being more publicly involved in denouncing the junta and not doing more to support a democratic Greece. Noting that Nick's ancestors were from Crete, she reminded him that the island's residents had always been courageous fighters. She was, she said, "deeply distressed by his lack of interest." Nick conceded that the tempestuous Mercouri "raised Cain with him." The military stripped her of her citizenship and confiscated her property. When not in the United States, she would spend the seven years of the regime's continuance in France. After its demise and the return of democracy Mercouri's citizenship was restored. In the new government she would serve in Parliament and as Minister of Culture.

Congress plays at most a limited role in foreign policy, but that does not preclude foreign junkets. In August 1969, well into Nick's second term, the military regime was host to twenty-two congressmen, anxious to show its achievements in dealing with some of the country's problems. Nick did not join that group but he was in Crete at the same time as a speaker at the Chania International Conference on Technology and Society, held on the campus of the Mediterranean Agronomic Institute in Chania. Knowing that Nick would be in Crete, Maliotis asked the congressman to speak to the First International Pan Cretan Association Congress that was meeting in a Turkish mosque in Iraklion. The meeting was interrupted when Stylianos Pattakos, the vice-president of the military government and one of the colonels involved in the coup, entered with troops that began firing their guns. Fear gripped the assembled guests and when the archbishop was told to stay in his seat, Nick was asked what to do. He responded that the colonel, who reminded Galifianakis of Mussolini, should be invited to speak. So he was, and for about forty-five minutes he extolled the virtues of the military government. Later, Nick was invited to come to Athens to meet President George Papadopoulos. Nick agreed, but when the president offered to schedule a dinner in the congressman's honor, Nick refused. Congress had been called into special session, and its members were recalled. When the president insisted, Nick said he had no other option than to respond to the call from home. He was thankful that he had an excuse for not lending support to the military regime.

Nick was establishing himself as an independent voice in a delegation that had tended to move in lock-step. President Johnson was well aware that he needed to court Southern Democrats, so he sent an aide to approach Galifianakis on the subject of raising the debt limit, something that had repeatedly been done without support from the North Carolina delegation. Galifianakis responded that he would study the matter and let the administration know the result. When asked again, he said his study led him to conclude that the debt ceiling was a rather meaningless device that probably should be scrapped. He promised that he would vote in favor of the coming increase. Henry Hall Wilson, Johnson's legislative liaison, was pleasantly surprised when five other members of the state's delegation followed Nick's lead.

Nick with President Johnson

Galifianakis sent out a newsletter that was reprinted in some of the district's newspapers. He listed his votes, shared concerns with his constituents, and notified them of the offices he had established both in Winston-Salem and Durham and when and where there would be office hours in other counties of the district. The newsletters came frequently. In one, Galifianakis paid tribute to a district soldier who had been awarded a Bronze Star. In another, he described the glories of the nation's capital. In yet another, he detailed the legislative efforts that resulted in North Carolina being the second best funded state to supplement school programs for disadvantaged children. He was referring to the Elementary and Secondary Education Bill that brought substantial federal monies to state educational systems. He took the opportunity to tell his constituents that he would support a $600 tax exemption for parents of children in colleges or in a vocational trade school. To encourage a two-way dialogue, he sent a questionnaire that was also printed in the district's newspapers asking readers to express their opinions on matters of foreign and domestic policy by sending responses to him.

Six months into his service in Congress, Nick was forced to respond to charges levied by the other new congressman from North Carolina, Republican Jim Gardner. Gardner picked up a charge that had been made by Steele in the 1966 race and gave it much wider publicity. That charge was that the Durham antipoverty program, Operation Breakthrough, had been politicized to aid Democrats in their political campaigns. The assumption in the press was that Gardner was firing an initial volley in what would be a political contest between himself and Nick in the 1968 election, when congressional districts would be reapportioned and both men placed in the same district. The *Durham Morning Herald* gave the charges first page coverage with a banner headline usually reserved for more momentous happenings. It supplemented the extensive coverage with a cartoon that pictured Gardner breaking through the wall of his office into Nick's office with an Operation Breakthrough sledgehammer. Gardner said that Galifianakis was well aware of the charges during the recent campaign and did nothing about them. Nick said that the head of Office of Economic Opportunity (OEO), Sargent Shriver, had assured him that the charges were without merit. Getting poor people to vote, Galifianakis said, was a legitimate aim of the program. Gardner, who had an ability to garner press attention, responded that if Shriver condoned such political activity, he should resign. Put on the defensive, Nick asked the Civil Service Commission to investigate. The Commission found no violation of law in the charges.

Nick tried to be measured in his response to the attack on Durham's antipoverty program, but when Gardner's comments seemed to exacerbate racial tension in the city, Galifianakis struck back. He told Gardner to tend to his own affairs and stop interfering in the 5th District. Any concerns, Nick continued, should be addressed to the District's representative to avoid stirring the caldron of racial tension.

Galifianakis would come to feel that he was always in the midst of a run for office, forced to campaign in counties that had not been included in the district he represented in the last election. By July 1967, the redrafting of districts in North Carolina resulted in Durham being placed in the 4th District, making Nick the incumbent congressman of a district that now contained residents of four counties—Wake, Randolph, Orange and Chatham—that had not participated in his initial election. Rumors had Gardner moving to Wake County to challenge Nick for the House seat in 1968.

Summer riots in the inner cities of some of the nation's metropolitan areas had an echo in Durham in July 1967 when black residents, asserting their power, marched in the city. City officials became alarmed by the sporadic violence accompanying the march. The governor called out the National Guard, but then quickly recalled the men when no further demonstrations occurred. Various state newspapers publicized the grievances the demonstrations brought to the fore, and city officials, led by Mayor R. Wence Grabarek, agreed to meet many of the demands. The demands concerned how urban renewal was being handled, poor and dangerous housing, lack of enforcement of housing codes, the absence of recreational areas, and the arrogant attitude of whites toward black grievances.

Nick was not directly involved in the negotiations but he did meet with the mayor and tour the urban renewal areas to acquaint himself with the dimensions of the problem. After his tour, Galifianakis concluded that the problems that had led to the demonstrations were local problems that had to be solved at the local level.

Rather than backing away from the controversy with Galifianakis, Gardner exploited the racial tension in Durham and continued to capture headlines in the state's newspapers. He praised the National Guard for stopping any further violence and urged the OEO to deny any further funding to the Durham office. Gardner incurred the ire of Governor Dan Moore when he attacked the charitable North Carolina Fund (a non-profit designed to reduce poverty and promote civil rights in the state created at the behest of former governor Terry Sanford) saying it had become "a political action machine," but angry responses to his charges seemed only to fuel Gardner's efforts.

Gardner's charges brought Watts Hill, Jr., a prominent businessman and civic leader, into the public arena to dispute Gardner's many charges and to put a favorable spin on the recent racial troubles in Durham. Praising the work of Operation Breakthrough, Hill said a community periodically needs to be shaken up—that only with tension does needful change take place. He said that without the leadership of Breakthrough the recent disturbances would have taken a much greater toll.

One commentator concluded that Gardner's popularity was the result of his ability to capitalize on widespread North Carolinian opposition to a program that spawned "chiselers." Others saw Gardner's crusade against the antipoverty program gaining points with North Carolina voters and therefore injuring Nick in a future head-to-head contest with Gardner. An editorialist for The *Chapel Hill Weekly* said that that Nick's cautious, rational approach to controversy was ill-suited to the coming political contest and that Nick could not win a race against Gardner by sticking to the issues; he must engage his opponent.

Bill Connelly of Winston-Salem's *Journal and Sentinel* captured Nick's dilemma, one that forced him into a defensive posture. Not to be intimidated by Gardner, Nick in November 1967 voted in favor of the administration's anti-poverty bill, extending the life of the OEO for a year. Proving his pragmatic streak, he voted for an amendment to the extension that sought to suppress any political activity on the part of those funded by the program. Only one of two members in the North Carolina delegation to lend his support to the bill, Nick said that in "the final analysis I could not bring myself to cast a vote against people in need." His courage was bolstered by mail that largely supported the program. His support for OEO and for the Model Cities Act separated him from most of the North Carolina delegation, but brought him accolades from one state newspaper for putting aside the fear of a Republican challenge and "building a fairly constructive record."

In the fall, Galifianakis was honored by being asked to deliver the keynote address at the annual Vance-Aycock dinner that brought the state's Democrats together. Nick was advised to avoid mentioning President Johnson because his domestic policies met with little state support. When Nick rejected the advice and called upon his fellow Democrats to show respect for the man undertaking "the biggest, the most complex, and the most thankless job in the world," his remark was greeted by spontaneous applause. Referring to

Great Society programs, Nick said it "will take character to stand by programs that have just begun to change people's lives for the better." For the present, Galifianakis urged his audience to make sure that the Party's symbolic donkey is "shod in shoes that are honed to a fine edge with the sharp instrument of pride." Accusing the Republicans of leaving a gap between their words and actions as big as the gap between the nineteenth and twentieth centuries, he proposed changing GOP to GAP. Galifianakis urged unity among Democrats, saying that they should proudly proclaim their accomplishments and do "a skillful job of . . . calling the factions together."

Democratic Party chairman Tim Valentine, at the urging of Governor Dan Moore, had chosen the young congressman to give the keynote address with the hope that he would energize a party prone to factionalism and complacency in the state. When Galifianakis ended his speech by inviting young people to join the party, whether as voters, workers, or candidates, to add their contributions to what "has given our party renewed strength and vigor for the past 175 years," the consensus was that he hit just the right note.

The unexpectedly large attendance, estimated between 1,000 and 1,200, was a record for the fund-raising event. Such large numbers help explain the problems Nick and his wife encountered prior to the dinner. When they arrived at the hotel, they were assigned a room on the eighth floor. Only one of the elevators was working. and crowds were waiting to get to their rooms. Nick decided that they would walk. After eight flights, when he opened the room, it had no beds. It had been cleared to act as one of the gathering's reception rooms. Eventually, a room with a bed was found on the sixth floor and the exhausted couple could relax.

Galifianakis' first year in Washington was one of considerable activity, but Nick was convinced that it prepared him well for the challenges ahead.

Nick, with his wife, Louise, being honored at a function.

INTERLUDE 8

Washington Politics

Two episodes early in Nick's congressional career suggested that the rose-tinted glasses through which he viewed political service might just need some adjustment.

The first concerned Frank J. Brasco, a first-term congressman from Brooklyn, New York. Nick's personality often attracted people, including his new colleagues in Congress who seemed intrigued by the fact that the young man had been elected from a Southern state. As Galifianakis and Brasco got acquainted, the New Yorker asked Nick who his sponsors were. This question puzzled the man from North Carolina. Brasco explained that he was asking who was responsible for putting him in his present office. The explanation did not help Nick, who said that the people of the state had put him in office. Either this response now puzzled Brasco or simply convinced him that this Southerner was especially naive. At any rate, Brasco, who was always well dressed, said, in response to a compliment from Nick, that the shoes were given to him by one of the companies in the district he represented. He asked for Nick's shoe size, and in a couple of weeks Nick had a new pair of shoes.

Nick's inkling that his new friend might be using his position not to serve the people, but rather special interests or himself, was borne out when Brasco was convicted for receiving payoffs from a trucking company seeking hauling contracts from the U.S. Postal Service. Brasco was disbarred and did not seek reelection.

The second episode hit closer to home and involved Howard Thomerson, the administrative assistant who Nick had inherited from retired congressman Ralph J. Scott. One day, Thomerson asked Nick what the charge would be for the congressman's nomination of candidates for the United States military academies. Galifianakis was taken aback, appalled that such nominations had previously been up for sale. He declared that from that time forward, no money would change hands with such nominations.

CHAPTER IX

A Busy First Term and Starting Another Campaign 1967-1968

While Gardner has been capturing headlines with his charges about political abuse by the Democrats of Durham's anti-poverty program, Nick had been busy working. He voted for legislation that would provide federal support for the training of the local police in riot control. The Riot Prevention and Control Act of 1967 became part of the Law Enforcement and Criminal Justice Assistance Act of 1967. He also supported legislation designed to help the urban poor with housing shortages. Furthermore, Nick had brought local officials together with high-ranking federal officials, including Vice-President Hubert Humphrey and Sargent Shriver, and was on the telephone endlessly with federal agencies seeking improvements in federal programs.

Galifianakis played an important role in the Banking and Currency Committee when he sought to introduce legislation dealing with the burgeoning credit card industry. Nick had been concerned with the lack of regulation of credit card issuers, which allowed them to hide exorbitant charges on credit card purchases and gave them the power to garnish wages to recover such debts. Some of his ideas were adopted without credit by the chairman of the Committee, Wright Patman and worked into Title I of the Consumer Credit Protection Act of 1968. As the bill was being reviewed, Nick informed Patman that the proposed bill had left out a section of Nick's suggestions. Patman said that the young congressman could propose an amendment.

This would give Nick some visibility in regard to the content of the legislation. However, when Nick sought to amend the bill Patman ruled him out of order. Apparently, the chairman was not going to give the freshman any public credit for the bill's provisions.

Nick voted against a proposal that would allow a 30% variance among congressional districts, the only one in the North Carolina delegation to vote against the bill. He defended his position by saying that such legislation would not be allowed by a Supreme Court that insisted upon a one-man-one-vote standard. A commentator found the vote "noteworthy because there is a growing belief that any redistricting plan drawn by the assembly will undertake major surgery on his district." Nick was honoring his convictions, preparing for a fight, and trying to counter Gardner's charges with action.

Nick's maiden speech in the House of Representatives on March 20, 1967 had concerned the war in Vietnam. Opposition to its continuance was increasing. Galifianakis recognized that his district was divided between persons who wanted to strengthen the war effort and expand the targets of military action, and persons who wanted an immediate withdrawal of American forces. As he would do in so much of his political life, he staked out a position in the middle. He urged Americans to support the progress that he saw and stand firm behind the American military commitment to ensure a stable, democratic South Vietnam. The optimism expressed by this freshman congressman would sour as the situation in Vietnam developed into a quagmire with no end in sight. With the Tet offensive beginning at the end of January 1968, the war showed no signs of being brought to a close and the rapid increase of American troops to well over 500,000 only encouraged requests for more. President

Johnson, with his ambitious Great Society program promising that the nation could have both guns and butter, was fast losing the popularity that had brought him the overwhelming political victory in 1964. It had dissipated to the point that Johnson announced on March 31, 1968 that he would "neither seek nor accept" the Democratic presidential nomination later in the year.

Nick making one of his many speeches.

As has been shown, Galifianakis was a talented speechmaker, and he rarely refused an invitation to speak if he was available. At one event in Durham he cautioned attendees at a Duke University medical seminar that the public was much concerned about where medical research was leading the nation. "There is no doubt," he said, "that the very boundaries of the human body and the human mind have been literally and figuratively trespassed. The public", he continued," needs to be reassured that medical advances, including an ability to modify the genetic makeup, will not lead either to standardization or further invasions of the human psyche." He also addressed a public affairs forum at Rockingham Community College where he suggested that a conference of Asian nations, similar to one recently held with representatives of Latin American countries, might well hold the answer to problems of Communist aggression.

Nick accepted so many invitations to speak at such varied forums for several reasons. First, he was much in demand and he enjoyed it. Second, it brought him in touch with his constituents. Third, it offered him free publicity in his many campaigns. Finally, he truly felt that he had important information to convey. When Congress was not in session, it was not uncommon for him to make as many as five speeches a month to groups ranging from students in elementary school to attendees at a scientific conference. In fact, at a meeting of a 4-H Club in which he detailed the way in which Congress works, he saw speechmaking as one of a congressman's duties. Generally, he relied upon his staff to put together the relevant material he would use in his speech, whether it was historical or simply a summary of congressional activity on the subject of the group's special interest. He then shaped and prefaced the material, often with some self-deprecating humor. A favorite beginning involved him telling the group how he had been introduced at some earlier gathering: "You all know the congressman. You've seen him plastered all over the district."

Although he could joke about himself and his role, he took his job very seriously and gave full commitment to its many dimensions. In addition to substantial committee work, speeches, formal votes, and informing constituents, he often gave testimony in hearings before House committees in which he had a special interest.

Because of the volume and efficacy of his work in his first year, Galifianakis was selected by a group of young Washington lawyers as one of ten Democratic members of the House that the lawyers would help get reelected. The group called itself Ten for Ten, Inc. Each of the ten lawyers worked with one of the congressmen, helping with research, position papers and even raising money. The congressmen were chosen with the following criteria in mind: "They had to have youth, geographical dispersion, divergent interests, liberal to moderate records, be Democrats, and not be secure in their home districts."

Nick's guardian angel in the group was Thomas H. Wright, Jr., a native of Wilmington, North Carolina and son of the Episcopal bishop of North Carolina. Wright had graduated from Princeton University and Harvard Law School and worked for one of Washington's prestigious law firms. In fact, he was largely responsible for Nick being put on the list of ten. The initial absence of Southerners on the list had spurred Wright to action, and, although Nick was the most conservative person on the list, he quickly won the approval of the other members of the lawyers' group.

Liberals may have seen Nick as conservative, but the conservatives didn't think so. As Nick's votes were tallied during this first year in Congress, he received the lowest rating of any North Carolina congressmen from Americans for Constitutional Action, a conservative organization designed to counter Americans for Democratic Action, a liberal organization. Senator B. Everett Jordan at 30% was a few points higher, while senior Senator Sam J. Ervin, Jr. received 92%. Republican Jim Gardner had a 100% rating. Although Nick would get some financial help from Ten for Ten, Inc. in his 1968 campaign, he saw its value largely in the brain power it contributed to getting "the cobwebs out of . . . [his] thinking."

TAX REVOLT BREWING

Not too long ago, the wire services carried a little news item which would have been a lot more amusing to housewives in the Fourth District had it not had such a distinct ring of truth. The news bit concerned a sign displayed in a Memphis business establishment which read: "T-Bones, 85 cents. With meat, $3.50."

This is about the most succinct commentary on increased living costs that I've seen. Unfortunately, the message in the Memphis window seems to have been lost on those who are not pushing the fight in Congress to bring relief to the average American taxpayer.

Recently I was quoted in the New York Times as saying that there is a middle-class tax revolt brewing in this country. I question that this is real news to folks who subscribe to the Times. I am certain it comes as no news to the vast majority of my constituents.

Realization that the average taxpayer's burden was quickly becoming intolerable led me early in this session of the 91st Congress to introduce a bill which would raise the personal exemption from $600 to $1200. I feel this one move would give more relief, and bring more reform, than any of the numerous measures which have subsequently been proposed.

Not only has the middle-income taxpayer seen his cost of living rise by 48 percent since 1948 — when the $600 exemption figure went into effect; he has seen his taxes increase astronomically.

One reliable tax source has indicated that all taxes to be collected in fiscal 1969 by federal, state, and local governments averages out to about $3,927 per American family. This represents a tax increase of $370 over last year.

I am told that tax receipts by the federal government alone have more than doubled since 1956, while state-local tax receipts will be close to tripling during the same period.

That's why I am placing such emphasis on my proposal to double the personal exemption. It's difficult to see how anyone can contend that a $600 exemption is equitable when one considers both the cost-of-living increase and the doubling of the tax.

In addition to this proposal, I am sponsoring a bill which would increase the amount of outside earnings by Social Security recipients from $140 to $250 monthly, and another bill designed to increase the standard income tax deduction from 10 to 15 percent, and to increase the ceiling on such deductions from $1000 to $3000.

I am hopeful that by late this summer Congress will have taken meaningful steps to bring relief to the lower and middle income taxpayer. There have been enough promises of relief. The time has come to take action.

BILLS INTRODUCED

- H.R. 4445 — Creating an agency to supervise Federal credit unions.
- H.R. 7989 — Extending Federal benefits to state and local law enforcement officers and firemen killed or injured in the line of duty.
- H.R. 8938 — Increasing the standard Federal income tax deduction from 10% to 15% or $3,000.
- H.R. 10812 — Protecting the rights of civilian employees of the Federal Government and preventing unwarranted government invasions of their privacy.
- H.R. 11076 — Permitting Social Security recipients to earn $3,000 outside income rather than $1,680 which is presently allowed.
- H.R. 11113 — Granting "combat zone" tax exemptions to servicemen currently on duty in Korea.
- H.Con.Res. 243 — Calling for an international conference to establish uniform territorial sea boundaries throughout the world.

One of the newsletters Nick sent to constituents

In addition to the newsletters that he sent directly to his constituents, Nick created a weekly summary of his congressional activities, called "Nick's Notes," that he sent to newspapers in his district. Those columns were themselves supplemented by news releases churned out by his office staff. All in all, the written record recorded the busy life of a committed congressman. Senator Sam Ervin, Jr. helped by inserting a number of generally complimentary newspaper articles into the *Congressional Record*, prefacing their entry by complementing Nick on "his untiring industry, ready grasp of the issues, and courageous action," which, he continued, had "earned for him the highest respect of his colleagues." As with his first term in Raleigh, Nick proved to be a fast learner, equipping himself to play much more than a nominal role in the nation's legislative process, even with the distractions provided by Garner's charges.

Nick made his office into one that got things done. Whether getting an old soldier the medals he had earned or responding to students' request for a flag, Nick realized that a key to future political success was found in responding to the needs of constituents. Harold Thomerson, the longtime legislative assistant, said: "I've never seen a man adapt to this job any faster than he has." One of Nick's colleagues added that "Within the limits of what a freshman can do up here, I'd say he has made an outstanding start."

By the time Nick had to campaign for reelection, the predictions that Durham would be detached from the 5th District and become part of the 4th Congressional District had come true. Despite the fact that Forsyth County would no longer be in his district in the coming election, Galifianakis continued to serve those constituents, causing a local newspaper to single out this attention as something quite special.

Newspapers were often in his corner. The *Charlotte Observer* had lamented what it assessed as the poor work of the North Carolina delegation in Congress, noting that only Nick Galifianakis had supported two important urban programs, the Model Cities Program and the continuation of President Johnson's antipoverty campaign. In each case, only one other North Carolina congressman joined Nick in support. The *News & Observer* in Raleigh praised Nick for "both an open mind and an honest one." Although such a mind may not be "a novelty in the Congress," the newspaper continued, it certainly reflects "credit on any freshmen legislator from any district."

Bill Connelly of the *Winston-Salem Journal* was intrigued by the man who had had "no honeymoon with voters and no respite from political warfare," yet still maintained his enthusiasm for his job. Connelly interviewed a number of congressional veterans, who had words of praise for the freshman legislator. Commenting upon a bill introduced by Nick seeking to impose federal penalties on credit card misuse, one colleague said: "A lot of guys spend years here without introducing something as timely, and necessary and well-conceived as that." The reporter noted that Galifianakis had brought with him legislative skills honed in Raleigh that he now applied to Congress. He "knows how to 'get along' in Washington," the writer continued, "partly from his instinctive friendliness and partly from his knowledge of how the system works."

The reporter looked ahead to the election in 1968 as a "tough battle," since Durham County was now joined with Orange, Chatham, Randolph and Wake Counties to compose the 4th Congressional District. It was a much more contiguous district, but it would require Nick to campaign in four counties in which he had no prior political organization. With Wake and Durham in the same congressional district for the 1968 election, a further obstacle for Galifianakis was the possibility that he would have to face Republican Jim Gardner. Gardner was the one North Carolina politician who rivaled Nick's ability to generate publicity. In fact, Gardner, just three days into the 1967 session, had broken with precedent that called for freshmen congressmen to stay out of the limelight when he called a press conference to criticize President Lyndon Johnson's State of the Union address. This early foray was followed up with further attention-grabbing action, so that in late March the *Greensboro News* ran a story with the headline "Rep. Gardner Outdraws Colleagues at Publicity Pump." Speculation that North Carolina redistricting would lead Gardner to challenge Galifianakis for a congressional seat in what was now the 4th District was countered by rumors that Gardner was using his perch in Washington to pave the way for a gubernatorial run. With 1968 forecast to be a Republican year and with Gardner's style of campaigning creating problems for Nick, one might well imagine how relieved he was when Gardner chose to set his sights on the North Carolina statehouse. Shortly after Gardner announced that he would be a gubernatorial candidate, Nick announced for the 4th District seat.

Despite the fact that his district contained four new counties, Nick had considerable visibility in both Wake and Orange Counties. Of course he had served three terms in the state legislature in Raleigh, Wake County's largest city, and had received considerable attention in capital newspapers. Voters in Orange County, the home of the University of North Carolina in Chapel Hill, one of the most liberal counties in the state, would find Nick quite acceptable. As with Duke University, Galifianakis had seen that the university had received its fair share of federal grants. Despite the challenge posed, he felt comfortable with the joining of Durham and Wake counties, noting that both counties shared interests in the Research Triangle Park and in the Raleigh-Durham airport.

His opponents in the Democratic primary, held in May 1968, were Charles R. Holloman of Raleigh who staked his claim to being "the conservative Democrat," and David W. Stith, the black president of a Durham business school. On the Republican side, Fred Steele was seeking another round with Nick, but this time he needed to win the Republican primary against a Raleigh businessman, William P. Garrabrant.

Nick fulfilled his promise during the primary campaign to travel to all of the counties, a much easier task than the one he faced in 1966. He also said he would open a full-time office in the capital city. With Forsyth Country no longer in his district, the office there could easily be transferred to Raleigh.

When Nick announced his candidacy for reelection, he said the key issues were Vietnam and racial unrest. In the campaign, Nick stressed his legislative experience and noted that in his first term he had traveled 41,000 miles back and forth from his district. A Harris Poll in January indicated that only 41% of the American people had a positive reaction to Congress, after three straight years of a clear majority coming to the same conclusion. Although negative feelings about Congress in general were rising, people at the local level tended to be satisfied with their own choices.

That proved to be the case in the Democratic primary where Nick had a much easier contest than the one he had with Bagley two years earlier, Galifianakis won the Democratic primary handily with almost 66% of the vote, outpolling both Stith and Garrabrant, who each garnered only about 17% of the vote. Steele disposed of his Republican challenger with equal ease, setting up a rematch, but this time in a district in which Steele believed he could get more than the 48% of the vote that he had won in 1966.

The campaign staff that Galifianakis had assembled for the 1968 campaign profited from the 1966 campaign and was now much better organized. Of course, the least organized and most inclined to ignore the schedule was the candidate himself. Nick let others worry about schedules, and for the most part his aides, with persistence, were successful in seeing that the candidate, while not always on time, met the demands of the schedule.

For Nick, the secret of electoral success was his tireless personal campaigning. He personally passed out many of the 80,000 brochures that the campaign printed, along with a substantial portion of the twenty-one cases of candy buttons the campaign ordered. In addition, the campaign put his poster on twenty-five billboards in the district and ordered 25,000 two-part campaign buttons. The buttons were quite popular and are still sought by political campaign button collectors. Almost $5500 was spent on such material during the 1968 campaign along with $4000 for newspaper ads. The cost for the Durham campaign headquarters, which opened a month before the election, was $2,263.47. The campaign's biggest expenditure was for television advertising, which cost almost $12,000. The commercials aired on stations in Raleigh, Durham and High Point. Most of these campaign ads ran in the last two weeks of the campaign. Radio spots, which began earlier, supplemented the TV ads. In these radio spots, local citizens usually spoke in sessions lasting no more than a minute. For one ad, though, the campaign was able to get Rod Serling, his voice familiar to audiences because of his hosting of the popular TV show, *The Twilight Zone*.

In the fall of 1968, Sophie Galifianakis, Nick's mother,

Campaign headquarters in Raleigh.

continued to aid the campaign with her supply of Greek pastries. Three of Nick's brothers, Pete, Mike and Harry, were also active campaigners, especially in the last week before the election.

Nick was momentarily slowed down with an infection and hospitalized on October 9, but by October 16, was resuming his hectic schedule. During his enforced absence, his speaking engagements were taken over by Representative David Pryor from Arkansas. Pryor denied the charge that Galifianakis was a liberal and therefore not truly representative of the majority of the population of the district.

Nick helping the Kiwanis club raise money for children's programs. (The word bubble was included on Nick's original copy of the photograph.)

The fellow congressman attacked the practice of labeling politicians like Nick who, he said, voted as the merits of the legislation dictated, not on the basis of any agenda, liberal or conservative. Nick must have appreciated this support because he always thought of himself as an independent thinker.

Galifianakis' opponent in the general election, Republican Fred Steele, ignored the facts and sought to characterize Nick as a puppet of the Johnson administration. Lyndon Johnson's forceful support of civil rights had undermined much traditional Southern support for Democrats. Randolph County, now a part of the district, was a Republican stronghold, giving Steele hope that the result this time would be different than in 1966. Nick's problem was not only a general Republican resurgence but also the difficulty in satisfying the diverse groups in the district.

As October waned, Steele attempted to give some substance to the charge that Galifianakis favored the administration's agenda over that of voters in the district. His evidence was Nick's vote against an amendment to the Export-Import Bank extension bill that would have prevented monies from being used to build an automobile plant in the Soviet Union. The Republican argued that this "one vote alone" was conclusive proof of the charge. Galifianakis quickly responded by saying that the record proved that he voted for the amendment, which indeed did become part of the law, on three separate occasions. Steele countered that his charge related to votes in the executive session of the Banking and Currency Committee on the amendment alone. On two occasions, Nick did not support the amendment. The controversy degenerated and Steele called Galifianakis a liar. Nick said that he and Steele were talking about different votes. Nick explained that his negative votes in committee were cast because of his belief that the amendment was too broad in that it prevented the bank from financing any project in a country with "Communist leanings." When the amendment was modified and included in the extension legislation, Nick voted for it, as he had initially indicated.

Steele said the issue was not that Nick was insufficiently opposed to communism but rather that the congressman was so aligned with an administration that opposed the amendment that he voted against the wishes of his constituents. Steele said that Galifianakis' contempt for the people who sent him to Washington was obvious. Nick, Steele added, tried to conceal these votes by referring initially to votes on the main legislation itself, not the amendment. The Republican pledged that "if I am ashamed of a vote I cast, then I will resign from office."

Nick was incensed that his integrity had been questioned, but he realized that his opponent was trying to get an edge in a close race. Some of Steele's supporters took to pasting "Beat Nick" signs over Nick's campaign posters. In addition, Steele sent out a six-page brochure indicating how he would vote differently from his opponent, though three of the nine measures involved raising the national debt ceiling. To the Republican emphasis on the need to restore law and order to a troubled society, Nick pointed to his support of the Omnibus Crime Control and Safe Streets Act passed by Congress. Clearly, Nick was being politically challenged in the new district where Steele was now tapping into a growing anti-administration sentiment in part revealed through North Carolina's growing support for George Wallace, the Independent Party candidate segregationist candidate.

Galifianakis had won his 1966 race because of overwhelming support in his home county of Durham, but now with both candidates from the county, the vote there could be expected to be more closely divided. Furthermore, only Durham County remained from Nick's prior constituency. Randolph County was clearly in the Republican camp, but the remaining counties, Wake, Orange and Chatham seemed to be narrowly in the Democrat's camp.

Nick was running hard, well aware that his incumbency in the 5th District was not much of an advantage. In fact, his votes in Congress provided targets for an opponent who had no record of his own for Nick to counter-attack. In an extensive interview by Raleigh's *News & Observer* Nick continued to stress his experience and to move to the right, agreeing with Republicans that the major issue in the 1968 election was the need to reestablish law and order in American society. He also argued that freedom of choice plans met the requirements of the Civil Rights Act of 1964. Nick promised that, as a member of the House, he would follow the wishes of the majority in his district if placed in the position of having to determine who among the presidential candidates he would choose if no candidate received a majority of electoral votes. On the issue of gun control, Nick said that the limit placed by Congress on mail order sales was sufficient for the time being, given his belief that gun control was generally a matter for local control. He said he would work to gain the release of funds for research at the three major universities in his district and again took the position that more research was the answer to the heath problems that tobacco posed. Nick said he would seek to reduce the welfare rolls and welfare amounts and concentrate on providing good jobs for the prior recipients.

Responding to his opponent's criticism of his support for the administration's spending policies, especially in regard to antipoverty programs, Nick said that he had supported less than half of the administration's bills and had attacked the anti-poverty program as poorly administered. He avoided commenting on the draft, a target of campus protesters throughout the nation. With regard to the Vietnam War, Galifianakis said he was in favor of halting all military action should Hanoi agree and allow the agreement to be supervised by the United Nations. He said one problem was that Hanoi was "having great difficulty on how to save face."

Despite—or maybe because of—the seriousness of the challenge he faced, Nick added to his arsenal of campaign gimmicks a jingle that was remembered long after the campaign itself faded from memory. In fact, a quarter of a century later Vivian Harris, a resident of Durham, recalled among her "childhood memories . . . walking around Holloway Street School singing Nick's campaign jingle: 'N is for Nick, Nick Galifianakis, I is for his integrity, C is for Congress, K is keep him there, we need Nick in Washington, D.C.'" And Ms. Harris was far from the only one whose memory readily brought the jingle to mind.

The catchy tune attracted youngsters who could not vote, but the 1968 election would see many more voters going to the polls than was the case two years earlier, largely because it was a presidential election year. There would be no incumbent because Lyndon Johnson decided not to stand for reelection. He could not figure a way out of the Vietnam quagmire and did not want to be remembered as the first president to lose a war.

In the 1968 campaign, Richard Nixon had been politically born again as the Republican presidential candidate. After the devastating defeat suffered by the Republican Party in Johnson's victory over the conservative Barry Goldwater in 1964, Nixon emerged as the moderate choice. He chose as his running mate Spiro T. Agnew, another Greek-American and the former governor of Maryland. Noting the common ancestry, before a speech in Detroit, Nick had been introduced as Spiro T. Galifianakis. He responded that his national political career antedated that of "Zorba the Veep," a reference, of course, to the popular 1964 motion picture, *Zorba the Greek*. Sentiment in the local Greek community, numbering about 750, ranged widely as some Greek-American Democrats considered the possibility of voting the Nixon-Agnew ticket.

Clearly other North Carolina Democrats also found the Republican ticket more attractive than its rival. When President Johnson decided not to be a candidate for reelection, his decision had left his vice-president, Hubert Humphrey, the frontrunner for the Democratic nomination. Humphrey was challenged by Senator Robert Kennedy, brother of the late president, John. But the senator's assassination on June 6, 1968 gave Humphrey the Democratic nomination. Humphrey, a long-time liberal, now was also burdened with the Vietnam War. He had little support among Southern Democrats. If a large number of North Carolina Democrats now deserted their party to vote for the Republican ticket, that did not bode well for Galifianakis' run in the new district.

Back on the campaign trail, Nick faced questions about his support of the Democratic presidential candidate and present vice-president, the liberal Hubert Humphrey. The 4th District candidate responded that party loyalty simply dictated such support. Steele continued the assault with posters that promised that he "Will Represent *You* in Congress!" In the posters "you" was always emphasized. Embodied in the attack was an idea that would be repeated by opponents in subsequent races—that voters could not trust a person with a name like Galifianakis to be their voice in Washington. Newspaper ads hammered away at the linkage of Galifianakis with Johnson and Humphrey. One ad carried the banner "Hubert Humphrey Needs Nick Galifianakis . . . But *You* Need FRED STEELE."

Fortunately, however, district elections are more isolated from national elections than statewide elections, a fact that aided Nick's electoral chances. Steele attacked Nick's voting record and tried to tie him to Humphrey, but Galifianakis had been a visible congressman, even to those people in the new district. He had strong support in Durham County, especially from the Durham Committee on the Affairs of Black People, along with the University community in Orange County.

Nick had beaten Steele in 1966 by a margin of over 5,000 votes out of a total of almost 80,000. Now the vote total was expected to be almost twice as large, as much as half coming from the new district's most populous county, Wake. The actual number totaled over 150,000 votes. Despite the fact that the Republican presidential ticket carried the state, the first time that had happened since Republican Herbert Hoover ran against Democrat Al Smith in 1928, Nick was reelected to Congress. When the votes were totaled, Galifianakis had won by a little more than 4,000 votes. Steele won Randolph County, as expected by a little over 5,000 votes, but Galifianakis won the other four counties by margins ranging from almost 3,800 in Durham to 650 in Wake. If the result was not a ringing endorsement of Nick's record, he was heartened by the fact that he had survived in a contest that he knew would be close. The unpopularity of the national Democratic ticket was demonstrated by the fact that Wallace outpolled Humphrey in the state.

With a second term secured, Galifianakis could for the moment turn his attention back to the job he was elected to do.

INTERLUDE 9

The Chairman and the Chairman's Chauffeur

In the state legislature, Nick had quickly risen to a position of some prominence, but on the larger congressional stage, newly elected representatives had little influence. For instance, one of Nick's early goals in Congress was to raise the federal tax exemption. He made little headway in his first term. However, what he had done in those first two years was not only get acquainted with his powerful colleagues, but also with support staff. Initially, this was less the result of any strategy than it was a part of Nick's gregarious and truly democratic nature. Early in life, he came to the realization that status was what divided people, and although his enjoyed his own status, it never separated him from others. Instinctively, he had created in Washington his own "kitchen cabinet". He took to heart the proposition that all persons were to be afforded equal respect and attention, whether they were a committee chairman or the chairman's chauffer.

The chairman of the powerful Ways and Means Committee was Wilbur Mills of Arkansas. Because of his position, Mills received considerable press attention. Nick was brought into this limelight when The *Washington Times* speculated that a future Democratic ticket might well be Wilbur Mills for president and Nick Galifianakis for vice-president. Nick had also become well-acquainted with Mills' chauffeur, who was so impressed with the young congressman that he claimed the North Carolinian as his own personal representative. When the chauffeur agreed with Galifianakis about the need to increase the personal

income tax exemption Nick unknowingly gained an important ally. With his chauffeur's support, Chairman Mills made
an increase in the personal exemption a part of the Ways
and Means' Committee's agenda.

Mills' political career did not have as happy an end as
it might have had there been a Mills-Galifianakis ticket. In
early October, 1974 U.S. Park Police had stopped a speed-
ing car with no lights. A woman hopped out of the car and
headed for the Tidal Basin. Mills, who was drunk, had tried
to stop her. She was a stripper stage-named Fanne Foxe, referred to as the "Argentine Firecracker." Both she and Mills
were married, but not to each other. They had been carrying on an affair since July, 1973. The tawdry episode did not
prevent Mills' Arkansas constituency from reelecting him
for the nineteenth time. However, when in late November,
1974, after the election earlier in the month, Mills appeared
with Fox on the stage of the Pilgrim Theater, a burlesque
house in Boston, the end was near. After Mills held a news
conference in Fox's dressing room, the House leadership
stripped Mills of his chairmanship of the Ways and Means
Committee. The long-time Arkansas representative did not
seek reelection in 1976 and later confessed: "I drank booze,
and I mixed drinks with some highly addictive drugs."

CHAPTER X

The Second Term, Third Campaign and Third Term
1969-1972

As the 91st Congress assembled in January 1969 with Nixon as president and Democrats in charge of the House and the Senate, Galifianakis continued to seek an increase in the personal tax exemption, a matter that had attracted his attention back in the North Carolina legislature. Now he focused on the $600 federal exemption, seeking to double it to $1200. To him the reason for the change was obvious in that the exempted amount bore no reasonable relationship to the actual cost of living. In Chairman Mills, he now had a powerful ally.

The present income tax dates back to 1913, when a constitutional amendment provided the authority for the federal government to tax incomes. The initial personal exemption was $3,000, or $4000 if married. In today's dollars, that initial amount would translate to over $70,000 and about $94,000 respectively. American participation in the First World War increased the need for revenue, and that need meant that the number of taxpayers had to grow. So, in 1917 the exemption was sliced to $1000 and $2000 respectively, but with what was then called a credit of $200 for each dependent. In the midst of the Second World War the exemption was $500 for the filer and each dependent. This last change transformed the federal income tax system, as the number of Americans paying income tax rose from 7.1% to 64.1%. The exemption amount per filer and dependent was set at $600 each in 1948, and there it would stay until the Tax Reform Act of 1969 implemented a gradual increase. The Senate was willing to raise the amount to $800, but the compromise with the House was a staggered increase to $625 in 1970, $675 in 1971 and $750 in 1972.

With the beginning of his second term in the House, Nick, momentarily free from controversy and redistricting concerns, became a much more active legislator. He proposed legislation that would deny foreign assistance to countries that had not acted in good faith to stem the flow of drugs into the United States, and that would protect ocean mammals and regulate the discharge of pollutants into the oceans and the navigable waters of the United States. On three separate occasions over the next couple of years, he would vote to give the president the power to impose wage and price controls to stem inflation. He also consistently supported measures designed to aid veterans.

Nick with his friend and colleague, Congresswoman Shirley Chisholm (an eventual presidential candidate).

One of the most contentious issues in the continuing battle to integrate schools in the South, as well as the nation, was the need for busing to break down the effect of neighborhood segregation. Nick continually had to fight off political charges that he supported busing. So, in February 1969 he introduced a bill to protect neighborhood schools and prevent massive busing. The proposal did come up for votes throughout late 1969 and early 1970, and Galifianakis dutifully cast his vote each time for the bill. The matter, however, would eventually be transferred from the legislative to the judicial arena where limits were placed on the reach of a pro-busing decision involving the Charlotte-Mecklenburg schools.

Any representative from North Carolina had to pay attention to two important economic interests, textiles and tobacco. With regard to textiles, Nick was one of the first politicians to foresee the dramatic effect that foreign competition would have on the domestic industry. He introduced legislation to protect the state industry from foreign competition.

The tobacco interest, running from agriculture through manufacturing, was even more important to the state than textiles. Tobacco was an agricultural product, and Nick in Congress consistently supported federal aid to agriculture generally. With regard to tobacco, Galifianakis introduced a measure to extend a restriction placed on the Federal Communications Committee (FCC) from banning cigarette advertising on radio and television. Whatever one's personal beliefs, no representative from North Carolina could neglect the tobacco industry without political fallout. Nick never denied that cigarettes might be harmful; his answer was to put money into research to produce a safer product. The tide was moving in the other direction, though. Money was being funneled into education to encourage the public to stop smoking. Galifianakis believed that such money could be better spent by investing it in research. People, he said, should be able to smoke without endangering their health or the health of others. His hope was that the harmful ingredients in cigarettes could be identified and then eliminated. The answer he felt could be found if sufficient monies were devoted to research instead of being spent on anti-tobacco advertising. But Nick, who argued that censorship was not the answer, was on the losing side when the FCC in 1970 banned cigarette advertising from radio and television and Congress passed a law providing for a health warning on cigarette packages. In response, Galifianakis and Senator Ervin joined in proposing a center to research lung cancer in North Carolina but without success.

Easing the sting of defeat on the tobacco issue, Nick was especially pleased to be the congressional representative at the launching of Apollo 11 at the Kennedy Space Center in Florida on July 16, 1969. The center had been named in honor of President John F. Kennedy whose promise was fulfilled by the moon landing on July 20. Louise Galifianakis, who had accompanied her husband, said the lift-off was the most amazing minute in her life.

Back in Washington, Galifianakis, through his newsletter, continued to urge his constituents to visit his offices and make their needs known. He said he and his staff answered about 1200 letters a week, some from individuals in counties he did not even represent. Part of his desire to make sure the lines of communication stayed open stemmed from a recent visit with constituents, which he said had convinced him that a middle class revolt was brewing.

As 1969 was coming to an end, Nick joined 278 other members of the House and 68 senators in signing on to an initiative of the Americans for Permanent Peace in the Middle East. They urged the Secretary of State and the administration to support face-to-face talks between Israel and her Arab neighbors and to resist any inclination to impose any settlement upon the parties. He sent another newsletter to his constituents that pointed to a new congressional scrutiny of military policy and spending. Galifianakis also noted that a proposed constitutional amendment eliminating the electoral college and providing for the direct election of the president had the support of both parties and, he believed, a majority of the American people. Similar proposals had found a stumbling block in the Senate. In the newsletter, Nick called attention to a growing concern that the U. S. mails were being used to distribute obscene material, and he indicated his support for a bill that would allow citizens to designate that they did not want to receive such material. (A measure to this effect, known as the Goldwater Amendment to the Postal Reorganization Act, became law in 1970.)

The end of the first year of his second term saw Nick honored in November in New York City by the Greek Orthodox Church for his service to the church over the years. At a ceremony heralding the first time a former Roman Catholic became an Orthodox bishop in the Western hemisphere, Nick was made an archon of the Ecumenical Throne of St. Andrew, the highest honor that the religion conferred upon a layman. It was given to those individuals who were distinguished by both their service to the Church and to their profession.

Although Nick's voting record was always more moderate than liberal, his opposition to the Vietnam War long before such a position became popular tended to strengthen the liberal characterization. He was the first person in the North Carolina delegation to take such a position and one of the first congressmen to take issue with the administration's conduct of the war. He came to share the views of Mo Udall and first term Congressman Al Lowenstein of New York, a University of North Carolina graduate and outspoken critic of the war.

Nick with Archbishop Iakovos of North and South America.

Nixon's announcement on April 30, 1970 that he had ordered troops into neutral Cambodia, thus widening the Vietnam War, spawned extensive student opposition on college and university campuses throughout the nation. When National Guard troops at Kent State University, ordered on campus by the Ohio governor, shot and killed four students and wounded nine others, a student strike closed institutions of higher learning across the country. On May 8 the Association Press reported that 224 colleges and universities had closed.

The University of North Carolina at Chapel Hill was in Nick's district and he paid close attention to the situation there. Students and some faculty protested the war and the killings at Kent State. Classes and final examinations were cancelled and instructors were authorized to determine grades on the basis of prior work. A candlelight vigil attracted 2500 students and a large contingent marched to Raleigh. When buses were charted to take some 600 students and faculty, led by student body president Tom Bello and law professor Dan Pollitt, to Washington, Galifianakis arranged a meeting with the North Carolina congressional delegation in a House conference room. After a two-hour meeting, only Nick and L. Richardson Preyer agreed with the students in condemning the invasion of Cambodia and in calling for the prompt withdrawal from Cambodia. Senator B. Everett Jordan said he would vote in favor of ending the war should a Senate vote be forthcoming. The rest of the delegation stood firm with the administration.

Individually, Nick spent an hour with the students who packed his office, after which he concluded that the students he saw were "no self-seeking group, and certainly not radical." The nationwide student protest calling public attention to the widening of the Vietnam war may have been a factor in the administration's decision to withdraw from Cambodia, beginning just a couple of weeks after Nixon had informed the public of the incursion.

On May 20, 1970 Galifianakis spoke extensively in the House on the need to set a timetable to end the American commitment in Vietnam. Although he said he was not taking issue with President Nixon, the congressman believed that peace talks in Paris were now unlikely to prove productive. Since the president himself had set a date for withdrawal from Cambodia, Nick believed that Congress should do the same, and bring the war of attrition to a close. Holding Nixon to his word of ending the war, Galifianakis said Congress could aid the president by setting a specific date for the withdrawal of all American troops. He set that date a little over a year hence, June 30, 1971 and proposed that all funds be cut off all by the end of that year. Nick also sought to limit presidential power by creating a Joint Committee on the War in Southeast Asia that would oversee the expenditure of funds to support military operations in Cambodia or Laos. Nick said that his position was a logical middle ground between those persons who sought immediate withdrawal and those proposing an immediate declaration of war.

Galifianakis' growing opposition to the war sat well with liberals on the university campus in Chapel Hill, but one area weekly newspaper felt that Orange County could do better than Nick, whose electoral success it satirically explained as the result of his "dogged moderation." From the *Anvil*'s perspective, Nick's continual sensitivity to political consequences led him to accumulate a "poor record." Yet even the paper realized that a district composed of "blacks, farmers, city folk, poor whites, campus liberals, conservatives, Republicans, old Southerners, recently arrived Northerners, and Democrats of all descriptions" with limited "natural alliances" was not easy to represent. In a number of votes Nick was either alone in the North Carolina delegation or joined by one other member. Most of these votes dealt with federal spending, which, generally, North Carolina's representatives sought to curtail. In a bill that passed the House, Nick joined the entire delegation in opposing a limitation of farm subsidies to $20,000 per person. What seemed to bother the left-leaning paper was Nick's opposition to a House attempt to ban single banks from owning commercial enterprises. Wachovia Bank lobbied against the bill, and Nick acceded to its wishes, while at the same time criticizing banks for credit card promotions that encouraged customers to borrow more money. With the 1970 election looming, the paper predicted that Nick would use the same political strategy to keep tobacco interests, campus liberals, and blacks in his corner, seeking to avoid any "ideological identity."

Nick was always comfortable speaking with young people.

The *Anvil* suggested that Nick would have more formidable primary opposition in 1970, and even if he was successful, a stronger Republican than Steele could emerge as a challenger in the general election. Although Nick did have seniority, his support for tobacco, and his pork barrel activity in his favor, the paper continued, he was vulnerable because he was not clearly conservative or liberal. This conclusion seemed to capture the tightrope that Nick had been walking to satisfy the diverse constituencies in his district and his own inclination for moderation. Its composition made the seat insecure, unlike so many other districts in the country where the incumbent was often invulnerable.

The political moderation that so disturbed the *Anvil*,

was well illustrated by an article in the *Congressional Quarterly*. The journal said that Galifianakis was one of only twenty-four congressmen "who have voted more than sixty per cent of the time against the positions of both the Americans for Constitutional Action and the Americans for Democratic Action—the right and left wings respectively of U.S. political thought." He supported desegregation but opposed forced busing, and with only one other member of the North Carolina delegation he voted for a continuation of the U. S. Civil Rights Commission.

Despite his differences with his colleagues in the North Carolina delegation, Nick liked them personally. They met regularly for lunch on Wednesdays, and after a while he did not hesitate to offer advice to his colleagues. Somewhat envious of their seniority, he urged L. H. Fountain and Alton Lennon to use it to their advantage. He even suggested how they might do this, for instance telling Lennon, since he represented the North Carolina coast, to develop an oceanographic initiative.

After one of those frequent visits home during the Christmas recess in early 1970, Nick identified inflation, which brought high food prices and interest rates, as the primary concern of his constituents. However, he could hardly neglect the issue of most vital interest to the young men in the district. Nick's antiwar position gave him support on his district's campuses, and he in turn saw that the campuses received a fair share of federal monies.

In 1970, the war issue impacted Nick's position in the U. S. Marine Corps Reserves, where he held the rank of major. In 1967, Secretary of Defense Robert S. Mc-Namara had sent a letter transferring Nick and four other congressmen to inactive status. The Secretary took the action in response to a group of veterans, under the banner of Reservists Committee to Stop the War, who believed that members of Congress who held reserve commissions were consciously or unconsciously biased in favor of the military effort in Vietnam. The veterans sought to force the 122 members of Congress who held such commissions to have them terminated. They based their claim, filed in the District of Columbia District Court, on the provision in the United States Constitution providing that "no Person holding any Office under the United States shall be a Member of either House during his Continuance in Office." The relief they sought from the Secretary of Defense and other plaintiffs was the striking of the names of all members of Congress from the reserve lists. Nick's response to McNamara's letter was a detailed defense of his contractual obligation to perform the service that, he said, took precedence over the Secretary's assumed authority to make such a transfer. To Nick's credit, the United States Supreme Court, using much the same reasoning that Galifianakis employed, would eventually decide against the claim that the constitutional wording precluded a member of Congress from continuing military service in the reserves. Nick continued in the Reserves and eventually was promoted to the rank of colonel.

Other battles would not turn out so well for Nick. In July, 1970 he came under the scrutiny of columnist Jack Anderson for his vote in the Banking and Currency Committee to gut a proposal made by Hyman Rickover, the admiral credited with the creation of the nuclear Navy. Rickover had convinced both the Comptroller General and the White House of the need for an amendment to the Multi-Bank Holding Company Act of 1966. It would have forbidden banks from owning commercial enterprises and would have better prevented defense contractors from padding costs. After intense lobbying by defense contractors, the measure was defeated 23 to 12 in a closed session of the committee. Anderson found Nick among the culprits who voted for the proposal's defeat.

Wright Patman, chair of the Banking and Currency Committee upon which Nick sat, had urged the committee to support the Rickover amendment and made public the names of twenty-one congressmen, including Nick, who had received contributions from the banking industry. Galifianakis denied having received any such contribution. Nick argued that his vote came from his conclusion that with the ban, banks would suffer unfair competition with other financial institutions.

Also, Drew Pearson, Nick's ally in his first run for Congress, now found fault with the congressman. In his contest with Bagley, Galifianakis had stressed his humble beginnings, but, Pearson said, Nick's votes on education, better housing, health and school lunches all supported cuts in these programs. Pearson further noted that Wachovia Bank, headquartered in the state, had been especially active in acquiring insurance agencies and was even going into the computer business, implying that Nick was protecting the bank's interests against reform attempts.

Then, on the eve of the 1970 general election, the Bankers Political Action Committee reported to the House Clerk that it had contributed some $55,000 to members of the House Banking and Currency Committee. Most of the named recipients denied receiving any contribution, including Nick, who the bankers group said had been given $2000. Galifianakis added that if he should ever receive such a contribution, he would "promptly return it."

Lost in this controversy was the passage of legislation,

coming out of his service with the same Banking and Currency Committee, that Nick had proposed early in his tenure in the House. Credit cards were becoming common currency in the latter 1960s without much in the way of regulation on the issuers. Nick's proposals were adopted without credit by Chairman Wright Patman, who first introduced a regulatory bill in August 1967. Congress finally passed legislation as an amendment to the Truth in Lending Act on October 26, 1970. The major provisions of the new legislation were a prohibition on issuing unsolicited credit cards and a $50 limitation on the liability of the credit card holder. With or without credit, Nick was pleased that he could face another reelection fight with this legislative success.

The change in the composition of congressional districts in North Carolina had been such a regular occurrence that Nick, in retrospect, believed that he ran each of his three congressional races in a changed district. This recollection was not accurate, for his 1970 campaign was waged in a 4th District that had not changed since its creation in time for the 1968 election. However, it was one of widely varying constituents and quite possibly representative of the nation as a whole in both its tensions and trends. For here in the district were three great universities and the constituencies that such intellectual centers inevitably attract. But the district was also home to tobacco farmers, well-organized blacks, rebellious students, and censorious adults. What attracted North Carolina voters to the Nixon candidacy was dissatisfaction with a rapidly changing society. Republican Herbert Hoover had won North Carolina's electoral vote in 1928, but that victory came largely on the basis of voting against his opponent, Al Smith, whose New York accent and support for an end to prohibition had alienated the state's voters. That vote was an aberration, signifying no real change in the state's politics. The Nixon victory in 1968, however, was a different matter.

One of the billboards used in Nick's campaign for Congress.

Fred Steele's two unsuccessful runs against Nick for a congressional seat had now left the Republican nomination in the district to others to contest in 1970. Both Russell Jackson Hawke, Jr. a 29-year old transplant from Pennsylvania, and Ben T. Perry, III, a businessman who had recently served as executive director of the Durham Redevelopment Commission, sought the nomination. Hawke had been active in the state's Republican party and ran Steele's last campaign before serving as an administrative assistant to Jim Gardner, the district's representative before Nick. There was little substantive difference between the Republican contenders on the issues, but Hawke was more politically savvy and used press releases and his organization to defeat Perry by a four to one count.

Nick's opposition to the continuing war in Vietnam made the upcoming 4th District election a possible referendum on the war, since the candidates took opposing positions. Galifianakis had won by only 4,000 votes out of the 150,000 cast in 1968, and Nixon had triumphed in his presidential contest with Humphrey, who ran third in North Carolina behind Wallace. Since the election, Nick had become "the leading dove in the North Carolina delegation," now calling for the withdrawal of American troops within a year. He supported the Cooper-Church Amendment to the Foreign Military Sales Act that would have barred funds from being used to continue the Vietnam War effort. Jack Hawke sharply criticized Galifianakis' position as tantamount to surrendering to the enemy. On college campuses where the opposition to the war was indeed strong, Nick would quip "I'm running against a real hawk." Hawke sought to gain traction with the old assertion that Galifianakis was soft on communism.

Vice-President Spiro Agnew was sent to campaign against his fellow Greek-American and bolster the Republican candidate's chances. Senator Sam Ervin not only was a visible supporter of Galifianakis but also the chosen person to counter the Nixon's administration support for Republicans. Hawke took the traditional Republican position of accusing Nick of being profligate, citing his votes to overturn President Nixon's vetoes on appropriations measures and noting that the Chamber of Commerce listed Nick as the only North Carolinian "big spender." Ervin responded that the votes concerned matters such as education, hospital and medical research matters, and water and sewer issues that could only make life better for North Carolinians.

Hawke also sought to link Galifianakis and the Democratic Party with the forced busing, although Nick had always taken a position against mandatory busing to meet racial quotas. The challenger noted, however, that Nick had failed to sign on to a friend of the court brief supporting the Charlotte-Mecklenburg School District in the case in which the U.S. Supreme Court upheld district-wide busing.

Campaigning with his wife, Louise, and young son, Jon Mark.

During the contest with Hawke, Galifianakis noted "the frustration of continuing . . . work as a congressman and having nevertheless to campaign." He compared his record in Congress with the relative inexperience of his opponent, who had never held elective office. And, as always, he relied upon what one reporter called his "most effective weapon... his personal charm, his wit, his informal ease with people. It works dramatically, and his furious-paced campaign is spreading it around like soft butter on toast."

As the election approached, Hawke revived the claim that Galifianakis had received a $2000 contribution from the Bankers Political Action Committee, BANKPAC, to advance its interests with the House Banking and Currency Committee of which Nick was a member. Nick had always denied receiving the contribution, and now E. D. Gaskins, the North Carolina chairman of BANKPAC, supported the denial by saying he had the check in his possession.

Although Nick lost some support among white blue-collar workers because of school integration, black militancy, and campus turmoil, his support from blacks, labor leaders and academics were expected to pull him through another tight political contest. Also Nick had outspent his opponent $30,290.17 to $22,891.78.

The race turned bitter in the waning days of the campaign, and it was midnight on election night before Galifianakis' supporters felt confident enough to proclaim victory. Nick again would lose Randolph County to the Republican, but by a much slimmer margin than in 1968. He eked out victories in the other four counties. With less than 100,000 votes cast, about a third less than in 1968, Nick had a little over 52% and Hawke a little under 48%, about a 4500 vote difference.

With the start of the 92nd Congress in January 1971, Nick finally got a post that he set his sights on after his first election to Congress: a seat on the House Appropriations Committee. Its membership had been increased to 55 from 51 to give to the Democrats the 3 to 2 ratio established by the new composition of the House, 254 Democrats, and 180 Republicans. Since the House Appropriations Committee was so involved with the federal government's budget, it had twelve subcommittees, which tended to make membership on this committee a full-time job. Of the six new members, four were classified as liberals, and two, including Nick, as moderates.

*Nick going to a meeting of the influential House Committee
on Appropriations between campaigns.*

As a member of the Appropriations Committee, Galifianakis got into an early battle with the president. Nixon had decided to impound funds appropriated by Congress, meaning he would not disburse monies that the legislature had authorized. Earlier presidents had impounded funds but only in situations where matters had changed so that the disbursement would not make sense. What Nixon did was take this precedent and use it to withhold money from programs that he opposed. A president could veto legislature that he opposed, but to withhold money from legislatively enacted programs raised a substantial constitutional question. Nick regularly proposed House resolutions calling upon the president to disburse certain impounded funds. At one time when he had George P. Shultz, the Director of the Office of Management and Budget before the committee, he asked whether the director was "willing to report to this committee whenever you withhold, or freeze, or defer appropriations, and tell us the exact nature of the freeze and the anticipated length of delay?" Shultz said he would have to consult with the president.

What eventually stopped Nixon was not the Appropriations Committee but Watergate. When Congress passed the Congressional Budget and Impoundment Control Act of 1974 that established a new budget process and provided for congressional control of the executive's impoundment of funds, Nixon was embroiled in the scandal and signed the act into law.

Galifianakis was especially active introducing bills in the House during the 92nd Congress's 1st session in 1971. For instance, he introduced a bill with 100 co-sponsors to provide survivors' benefits to firemen and policemen killed in the line of duty, a bill to increase federal funding for beach erosion, and a bill to fund free or reduced cost school lunches, among others. Had he represented one of those congressional districts in which reelection was a foregone conclusion, as was the case with most of his colleagues, he might have been quite confident of an indefinite future as a member of the House, but that was certainly not the case with North Carolina's 4th District.

Although Nick had been a consistent supporter of civil rights, he ran into trouble with the newly formed Congressional Black Caucus. The organization consisted of the thirteen black members of the House at the time. Its purpose was to alert black citizens to votes cast by their congressmen contrary to black interests. As its first action, the members chose the vote on a civil rights proposal in a fair employment enforcement bill. The bill sought to give to the EEOC strong cease-and-desist powers to combat job discrimination. The provision lost by five votes. The caucus singled out two congressmen for condemnation of their votes, representatives whose close electoral victory could be attributed to the support of blacks in their respective districts. One of them was Nick Galifianakis. Nick supported what ended up in the law which was to have cease-and-desist power entrusted to the courts rather than the commission, a natural place in his lawyer's mind.

Nick, however, had a good relationship with blacks in his district and went about as far in his support of civil and equal rights as a North Carolina congressman could. He voted to extend the life of the Voting Rights Act, a measure of great importance in finally breaking down the barriers to voting, especially in the South. He supported the Senate amendments to the extension that lowered the voting age to 18. When the United States Supreme Court said that the federal law could not cover state and local elections, Galifianakis supported the constitutional amendment proposal that became the 26th Amendment to the Constitution on July 1, 1971.

Nick was a supporter of access to opportunity for all. He co-sponsored and voted to send an Equal Rights Amendment to the states for ratification. The House went on to pass the resolution by a vote of 354-24. Not until March 1972 did the Senate concur by a vote of 84 to 8. Thirty-four states ratified the proposed Equal Rights Amendment, but despite two congressional extensions of time, it fell three states short of the constitutional requirement.

In his third term, Galifianakis became the key player in a legislative drive to relieve doctors of the obligation of their educational loans in return for practicing for three years in areas in need of medical help. There was a program on the books that forgave federal loans for doctors who agreed to practice in areas that were medically deficient, but only five individuals had taken advantage of the program in the seven years of its existence. He attributed this result to the overly restrictive legislation, which he now proposed to expand to cover not only federal loans but private loans as well. What had gotten Galifianakis interested in the matter was a problem in Fuquay-Varina, a small town in his district. Two of its four doctors had recently died, and the town found it difficult to recruit new general practitioners. Not only did Nick direct his staff to help find doctors for the town, he signed up 127 of his House colleagues to support changes in the loan forgiveness program. He calculated that the cost to the government would only be about ten million dollars a year.

On November 18, 1971 Galifianakis' initiative paid off as the medical shortage was finally addressed by legislation that had over 100 co-sponsors from both political parties, as well as support from the American Medical Association. Housed within Amendments to Title VII of the Public Health Services Act, the legislation consisted of the Comprehensive Health Manpower Training Act of 1971 and the Nurse Training Act of 1971. The first act provided for the cancellation of 85% of all student loans for physicians who practiced in physician shortage areas and provided grants for medical students who agreed to practice in those areas. The second act provided grants to nursing schools to provide new, advanced programs that would produce nurse practitioners, who could supplement doctors in providing needed medical aid.

With another election already on the horizon, Nick's voting record would be closely scrutinized. We have seen how people both on the right and left had criticized that record, something in which Nick, who practiced the moderation his father long ago preached, took some satisfaction. Tabulations of the votes of members of Congress have been done for various purposes, thus giving us a number of different perspectives on Nick's voting record. Perhaps the place to start is not with an organized interest group but rather with a loose but generally effective joinder of Southern Democrats and Republicans into a Conservative Coalition. In Nick's first year in Congress he voted with this group 85% of the time; only in 1971 when the tally was 54% for and 36% against was Nick more reserved in his support.

Despite a preference for in person contact, Nick spent considerable time on the phone.

Next we can take a look at party unity; that is, how often Nick voted as did the majority of Democrats in the House. President Johnson's civil rights and Great Society programs were not received with favor in most of the South, leading many Southern Democrats to vote against the president and the majority of their party. Nick supported Johnson over 60% of the time, but he also supported Nixon by similar margins in the first two years of Nixon's presidency. Only in 1971 and 1972 did the margin of support lesson. In regard to party unity, Galifianakis almost equally divided his support and opposition in his first year, 49% to 51%. In his second year the count was 39% to 49%. Then in Nixon's first three years, Nick's voted with the majority of Democrats from 56% to 63%. In his last year, 1972, he would oppose the Democratic majority more than support it.

The closest we have to interest groups with opposing points of view at this time are the Americans for Democratic Action (ADA) and the American Conservative Union (ACU). Scores only were tabulated beginning in 1971; in the two years Nick served he scored 35% and 19% aligned with the ADA, and 37% and 60% with the ACU. The National Education Association (NEA) started charting the votes of members of Congress in 1971, and in the first tabulation Nick only supported one of the three measures NEA pushed, but in the second tabulation he supported two of the three.

What all this confirms is Nick Galifianakis' self-characterization as a political moderate. Given his Southern constituency, despite its increasing dilution by Northern migrants, he was far from the liberal his conservative opponents pictured. But given most of the company Nick had in the North Carolina delegation he clearly deviated from its generally conservative line. Also, his political sense tempered his embracing ways, which, in a different political environment, would probably have led him to support Lyndon Johnson's vision of a Great Society with enthusiasm. And certainly he believed what some Southerners could never accept - that people of different races should be treated equally. He learned that lesson long ago as a youngster when his father tore down the partition separating the races in the Lincoln Café.

Both Nick's campaigning and his record won admiration from fellow representatives and the press. Senator Sam

Ervin, Jr. concluded that "Congressman Galifianakis does the best job of any congressman I know in representing the district." And Paul Clancy of the *News & Observer's* Washington bureau said that Nick "has shaken up the North Carolina political system" that had been characterized by "definite blueblood markings [where] family name and wealth [were aligned with] political power and influence." Despite or because of his baggy $50 suits and second hand cars, he continued, Galifianakis has "become a political leader in the state." Clancy attributed the rise to Nick's sincere interest in people, his friendly personality, and his wit and humor.

Despite his rise to a position of some power in the House, Nick saw a new threat to his House seat. The North Carolina legislature had once again reapportioned its congressional districts. Only ten of the hundred counties were shifted, but the one that mattered most to Nick was Orange County, the home of the University in Chapel Hill. Although a number of factors were pushing him in the direction of seeking the seat of North Carolina Senator B. Everett Jordan, this new redistricting led him to discuss the possibility publicly.

INTERLUDE 10

The Importance of Underwear and Connections

Galifianakis made responding to constituent requests a high priority, at times with amusing results. One day, Nick got a call from a political friend asking whether the congressman could arrange a meeting for executives from the Hanes Corporation with Mendel Rivers, the chairman of the Armed Services Committee. Rivers had been in the House for twenty years prior to Nick's arrival, and he proclaimed that he was the third most important person in the world. Still, he was susceptible to Nick's charisma, despite the fact that he kept making fun of Galifianakis' name and berating him as a liberal. Rivers pinned the liberal label on Nick because of the young congressman's fondness for smoking a pipe and reading the *New York Times*. Perhaps it was Nick's late-night walks with Rivers that solidified their friendship.

The Hanes executives were upset that their underwear was being replaced in prominence by a competitor's in PXs throughout the world, despite contractual assurances that the products would be given preference in all displays. Nick responded to them that he would get in touch with Rivers to see if a meeting could be arranged. One early morning, Nick went to Rivers' office and found the chairman quite receptive. When Nick asked when the meeting could be scheduled, Rivers said why not that afternoon? When Nick mentioned that might be too soon for the Hanes people to arrange travel, Rivers said the company must have its own planes. He was right. When Gordon Hanes was told he could have the meeting as soon as he could get to Washington, he boarded the company plane and arrived with two other executives in Nick's office by mid-afternoon. Nick personally introduced the Hanes contingent to the chairman. Rivers greeted them by pulling down his pants to show that he wore Hanes underwear. With this auspicious start, when Rivers was informed of the problem, he assured the men that their underwear would be restored to visibility in all PXs. And he made good on his word.

Although Rivers could be quite jovial, he could also be anything but. Nick saw the other side when he asked why the South Carolinian was not at the White House for the special showing of the film *Patton*. Rivers said he had not been invited. To add injury to insult, Nick also remarked that Drew Pearson, the columnist, had also been present. Rivers hated Pearson, largely because Pearson had written about Rivers' fondness for alcohol. When Rivers made his irritation with the White House known, an apology was extended along with an invitation to a private showing of the movie. However, it was not missing the movie that riled the congressman but his exclusion from a group that even included the young North Carolina congressman. Rivers refused the belated invitation.

CHAPTER XI

Toppling an Incumbent in the Democratic Senate Primary
1972

In the state's latest reapportionment by the 1971 General Assembly, Orange County was moved out of the 4th District, depriving Nick of the voters who had provided him with strong support in his two previous elections. Only Nick's seat seemed imperiled, as leaders from both parties seemed generally pleased with the redistricting. However, Galifianakis saw an unusual opportunity to move up the national political ladder and seized it. A six-year senatorial term would allow Nick to escape the constant campaigning that the two-year terms of the state legislature and the House of Representatives demanded for the past decade and concentrate on his legislative duties. It would also allow him to relocate his family to the Washington area. During all his time in the House, only one summer when he rented a house did his wife and children join him in Washington. The rest of the time he lived with a friend, Ned Everett, and travelled back home to Durham almost every weekend.

At age seventy-five North Carolina's junior senator, B. Everett Jordan, a Democrat, had decided to run for a third term. He had survived a colon cancer operation the previous year, a fact that led the political establishment to envision his retirement, not another campaign. Whether he would survive another six-year term was doubtful but not really a liability, given the fact that the state's senators had more often than not died in office. Their demise gave the state's chief executive the opportunity to appoint a successor, who would at election time have the advantages of incumbency. In fact, Jordan himself had been first appointed to the office in 1958. He had been a textile executive who had served as state Democratic Party chairman and was a national committeeman when selected by Governor Luther Hodges to fill out the term of Senator W. Kerr Scott. With no challenge within the party and no real Republican threat, the new incumbent had been assured of electoral success. The last contested election for the United States Senate in North Carolina was in 1952 when the former president of the University of North Carolina and appointed incumbent, Frank Porter Graham, was defeated in a bitter and nasty Democratic Party primary. With Jordan announcing his candidacy for a third term, those party stalwarts who coveted his seat were forced to the sidelines. One did not rise in North Carolina's largely one-party political system, with its unwritten but understood rules, by challenging an incumbent. Never fully embraced by the Democratic Party establishment, though, Galifianakis was not inclined to follow its unwritten rules, or even, for that matter, recognize that they existed.

In his congressional campaigns Nick always seemed vulnerable, yet he had won three times, if always by relatively small margins. Although he had regularly surprised the naysayers, taking on the incumbent Jordan seemed especially foolhardy. From Galifianakis' perspective, however, the time was right. His congressional district was again in flux; Jordan's incumbency had ruled out other serious challengers for the Senate seat; and a six-year term looked mighty appealing after the constant campaigning. Still he had to convince himself that an uphill battle for the Democratic nomination could be won.

When Congress recessed in early August 1971, Nick decided to tour the state and sound out support for a run for the Senate. In a twenty-six-day swing, he visited most of the state's one hundred counties. Warm receptions convinced him that he could win a state-wide race. Well before his tour ended, the general understanding was that he would become a candidate for Jordan's seat. That was the position taken by Roy Parker, Jr. in the *News & Observer*, who wrote as follows: "North Carolina, with fewer foreign-born in its population than almost any state, has a Jewish Miss North Carolina and soon will have a serious Greek candidate for the U.S. Senate ... who at the least was sure to add zest to the 1972 campaigns." The fact that his congressional district had fluctuated in its composition tended to give Nick a substantial base of support throughout the Piedmont. Jordan's strength would be in the more rural areas of the state.

A poll taken in mid-October 1971 predicted that the incumbent would beat the would-be challenger by a margin of 61% to 27%. Nick did not place much stock in polls, and at any rate, he had six months of campaigning to close the gap. Just how willing North Carolinians statewide were to embrace ethnic diversity, however, still remained unclear. Nick's formal announcement came on November 22, 1971, a little over five months before the primary election scheduled for May 1972.

In his press release Galifianakis said that as a first generation North Carolinian he felt "challenged" to be a part of the governing process, and that his service in both state and federal legislatures had only reinforced his belief that he was destined to devote his life to public service. Nick said that he would entrust the voters with determining which candidate "is better prepared to harness the potential and solve the problems of new technology and vanishing space, which have turned our planet into a single neighborhood." Problems concerning the environment, economy and national security, he continued, require new solutions if old problems are to be solved. He concluded with the following: "With the help of God . . . with the blessing of my mother and my brothers . . . and with the faith and support of the good people of North Carolina's 'Goodliest Land,' I believe I can meet the test of our new times."

An early supporter of Galifianakis' bid was Russell G. Walker, the founder of a supermarket chain called Food Line and a former N.C. state senator. Walker, who had served as Nick's campaign manager in the 1970 election for the House, resigned as chairman of the Randolph County Democratic Party to undertake again the challenge of running Nick's campaign.

Clearly, Nick felt that Jordan at 75 was vulnerable to a challenge by a man a generation younger. The age of the incumbent was a matter that had to be dealt with in a sensitive way, because a heavy hand might produce a backlash. When quizzed about the age issue, Nick normally responded that age was not an issue, saying instead that it was a fact. Jordan's press secretary confessed that Jordan's presence on the campaign trail was designed "to get maximum exposure of the Senator as a vigorous and active individual." Still Jordan made only a few stops each day, each time settling in and making himself available to those who came to him. In contrast, Nick's campaign was described as frantic and accompanied by "all the technology of the modern age: the camper that gets only four miles to the gallon, a machine that can copy messages over the phone, eight-track stereo, [and] a briefcase radio-telephone. It is a campaign in which the candidate seeks to engage others, to the extent of bursting onto a scene, whether courtroom or children's ward in the local hospital. He stays until all hands are shook or until he is thrown out." The commenter noted that Nick did not hesitate to talk about "our future," as he ran billboard ads in which he was joined by his 8-year-old daughter Katherine and his 5-year-old son Jon Mark. And to older voters who might identify more with Jordan, Galifianakis said "I can do more for senior citizens than a senior citizen can."

One issue did seem to work in Jordan's favor—his fourteen years in the Senate. Such seniority would be lost were the incumbent dislodged. Jordan's ads played the seniority card, saying that his years of service made him the nineteenth highest-ranking senator. They stressed the connection between seniority and federal benefits to the state, focusing on a piece of legislation that established acreage and poundage controls on tobacco that Jordan claimed had saved North Carolina's tobacco industry. To deal with both the issue of seniority and personal vigor, the incumbent's campaign said that Jordan served on more committees than any person in the entire Congress. Nick responded that the senator's seniority did not seem to bring much in the way of tangible benefits to the state.

As members of the North Carolina congressional delegation, Nick and Jordan got along quite well. In fact, Jordan's record, while not progressive, was certainly not a rigidly conservative one. Jordan was generally regarded as a moderate, though his coming out and demanding an end to the war in Vietnam was viewed by some as quite radical. Although Nick's opposition to the war antedated the senator's, Jordan claimed that putting an end to that war was his first priority upon being reelected. The fact that he and Nick, among the earliest Southerners to take a stand against the continued presence of the United States in Vietnam, saw eye to eye on the war created a kinship that fostered some restraint in the campaign that would be waged.

Jordan had campaigned for the office twice before and assumed that his campaign style was sufficient to defeat the new challenger. Galifianakis certainly did not underestimate the task that lay before him. Nick never said vote for me because I am young and vigorous, but observers got the message anyhow, reinforced by his ebullient personality. He would put in 18-hour days, from 6 a.m. to midnight and yearn for more hours in the day. Jordan, as any frontrunner would, refused to debate the challenger and was content to run a banker's hours' campaign, usually returning home every evening. Galifianakis was constantly on the go, so much so that his wife could say, without exaggeration, that she had seen him for only a few hours in weeks. He was a born campaigner who met new people and made them feel important. He was impetuous and rough around the edges and, to those in Jordan's camp, not really a substantial threat. Certainly their candidate could not match Nick's energy and stamina, but incumbency was a huge factor and their candidate had a visibility that Nick still had to gain. In a vigorous campaign, Galifianakis employed all modes of transportation—car, mobile home, plane, train, and helicopter—as he crisscrossed the state.

He also attracted talented staff. One of the volunteers who joined the campaign as a press and publicity aide was a graduate student in the University of North Carolina's School of Journalism. Jim Lampley would go on to make his reputation as a sports broadcaster on the ABC and NBC networks, especially with regard to coverage of the Olympic Games. Another addition to the campaign staff was Lance Brisson, a 1972 congressional fellow and the son of film and theatre producer Frederick Brisson and actress Rosalind Russell. Brisson quickly warmed to his assignment and gave Galifianakis some publicity with an interview published in the *Intellectual Digest*.

The piece was titled "Galifianakis & the Political Oligarchy," and Brisson questioned Nick on whether a candidate of limited financial means could succeed in a race for statewide office and whether relatively new technology had distorted the democratic process. Galifianakis answered yes to the first question and no to the second. However, he did agree that candidates were being packaged and there was a shift away from a focus on the candidate's character and qualifications. Nick said the use of the media was healthy if it informed the electorate, and unhealthy if it deceived. He recognized that in a short campaign an unscrupulous candidate could hoodwink voters by a blitzkrieg of false ads. His answer to this scenario was the unrealistic possibility that the House of Representatives, which can make its own rules, would nullify the election. His false hopes were further demonstrated when he said that contributors to political campaigns who claimed to be serving the public interest could support all by buying radio and television time and making it equally available to each candidate. Nick's expressed faith in the wisdom of the democratic electorate to see through the distortions and falsehoods of a well-financed campaign would be tested in the months ahead.

One of Nick's favorite modes of transport was a self-contained motor home, named Miss Sophie after his mother, that allowed him to travel the state. It was a gift from Davidson County supporters. It was air-conditioned, slept six, had a full kitchen, and a bathroom with a shower. Nick was convinced that his personal style of campaigning would offset his limited campaign chest. Furthermore, he believed that expensive media presentations could never compete with person to person contact. At other times, Galifianakis traveled in a donated Volkswagen camper, dubbed "Nick's Folkswagon," to barbecues and shopping centers where he charmed would-be voters.

The "Folkswagon" made Nick an even more agile campaigner.

Despite his best efforts, Nick could not be in all places in the state at all times. His wife, Lou, and his brothers, Harry, Pete, and Mike, who billed themselves as "seven hundred and fifty pounds of heavy campaign equipment," sought to fill the gaps. Somewhat proudly, Harry pointed out that Nick's campaign, unlike that of his opponent, was financed not by large corporate contributions but by small donations from many persons throughout the state. He also noted that the campaign was waged exclusively by volunteers with no paid workers on the staff. Headquartered in Raleigh, Nick's campaign manager Walker set up a campaign organization in each of the state's one hundred counties. Clearly Jordan had the support of the Democratic establishment, forcing Walker to build a rival organization relying on younger voters who responded well to challenging the status quo. When the *Greensboro Record* interviewed voters they found Jordan supporters saying things like "he has done nothing to make them dissatisfied." On the other hand, those who supported Nick noted things like his "fresh outlook," his "abundance of ideas," or his role as "more a man of the people."

Jordan's campaign stressed the value of incumbency and experience. Nick countered that he had more than sufficient political experience, adding that Jordan had not turned his incumbency and seniority into clout in the Senate. Nick pointed out that in more than a dozen years in Congress, Jordan had sponsored little legislation and had not used his position on the Senate Agriculture Committee to promote the state's interests, including protecting tobacco exports, at that time a major state concern. Jordan suggested that Nick was spending so much time campaigning that he was neglecting his responsibilities in the House. Galifianakis responded that he had made it back to Washington for the important votes. Jordan argued that he had outperformed the congressman in a number of areas, including the protection of the textile industry, flood control, and environmental legislation. And when the incumbent's campaign brought up the old charge that Nick might be too liberal for the state, Galifianakis pointed out that his record showed that he was one of twenty-four moderates in the House who voted over 60% of the time against initiatives from both the far right and the far left of the political spectrum.

Senator Jordan's son, John, was impressed by how Nick campaigned, saying "he used the press better than anyone I had ever seen." And when his father was in Washington working on a bill dealing with a North Carolina project, Nick went to the affected area and got the publicity. John Jordan concluded that the challenger was the press's darling because he was both quotable and affable. As early as March the *Concord Tribune* in Cabarrus County sported a headline that read "Galifianakis—is it becoming a household name?" The news editor, John W. Kennedy, noted that when Nick first visited the county a few months earlier he was largely unknown; now, Galifianakis was being greeted as a rising star. Nick continued to play upon his name, reviving the campaign buttons that he had first used in his House races, the ones that split his name into two parts, "Galifi" on one and "anakis" on the other.

Nick had been an early supporter of the 26th Amendment that enfranchised persons from ages eighteen through twenty, which had been added to the Constitution in the previous year. Estimates about the accretion to the vote in North Carolina ranged from 30,000 upward. Nationwide, the estimate was as high as eleven million. The general feeling was that these new voters might be more inclined to support younger candidates, especially when the gulf between ages was as great as it was in the North Carolina race. Jordan, who voted against the resolution sending the amendment to the states, still contended that a considerable number of young voters saw him as the better candidate. In a mock election at Lenoir Community College in which 600 students participated a few days before the primary vote, Nick not only thrashed Jordan by winning 71% of the student vote to Jordan's 26%, but he was the leader among all Democratic candidates. Clearly, the relative youth and matching enthusiasm of Galifianakis resonated much better with the newly enfranchised voters. This unscientific sample was corroborated in a new poll on the eve of the primary that indicated that Nick had indeed closed that large gap of the previous October and now seemed to have edged ahead of the incumbent Jordan.

Newspapers in the state tended to favor the challenger. The *Charlotte Observer*, however, refused to endorse either candidate, though it believed that Jordan "might be a more likely general election winner." It said Jordan was not much of a leader, appearing "contradictory and shallow on such matters as defense spending, education and poverty problems, civil liberties, foreign policy and other subjects of Senate concern which deeply affect us all." On the other hand, the paper, though seeing leadership potential in Galifianakis, was "disappointed in his campaign and in the fuzzy way he has addressed many issues during the past several years." The *Observer* concluded that the campaign of both men avoided the most pressing issues confronting North Carolinians, therefore leaving voters "to make a judgment more on matters of age and personality than on issues." Joe Goodman of the *Winston-Salem Journal* tended to agree that the campaign was "bereft of issues," saying that Jordan would only talk freely about his opposition to the war in Vietnam and his opposition to foreign imports, especially of textiles, saying that his committee work did not afford him the knowledge to comment on other matters. The reporter said that, although Galifianakis was willing to talk about all issues, his approach tended to avoid controversy, as he strove for moderation on all matters. Goodman concluded that instead of staking out clear positions, Nick "has promoted his own outgoing personality and his distinctive name." When it came time to make a choice, the *Journal*. while granting that the task was difficult, concluded by favoring Galifianakis on the basis that the "attraction of a youthful, vigorous new man is hard to resist." The *Charlotte News*, however, concluded that it was "wiser to gamble that Jordan will remain vigorous than to gamble that Galifianakis will grow into the job." The *Greensboro Daily News* forthrightly said that Jordan, given his age, should not have sought reelection, and then went on to endorse Nick as "a man equal to the challenges of the Senate." It said that its choice "has the capacities of mind and character to attain influence, if not eminence, in the Senate."

As the election approached, Nick stressed the need to further raise the federal personal income tax exemption. This was a matter that he had latched on to early in his political career, noting that both state and federal personal exemptions were still woefully inadequate. Galifianakis also hinted that Sam Ervin favored his candidacy, noting the positive remarks North Carolina's senior senator had made regarding Nick's service in the House of Representatives. Ervin had hoped he could avoid making a choice, but when both candidates claimed his support he had no choice but to go public. He followed the Democratic establishment's choice of Jordan, a decision that was hardly surprising. The obvious choice might also be the best personal choice should Ervin, only a year younger than Jordan, decide to run again in 1974. Clearly, many observers would read a Galifianakis victory as setting a precedent that increasing age was a political disability. During most of the campaign, Nick only indirectly called attention to his opponent's age, but few voters could miss his more direct aim when on the eve of the primary he suggested a compulsory retirement age for public officials between 70 and 75.

As the first primary neared, Nick also criticized Jordan for neglecting the state's tobacco farmers. Galifianakis introduced legislation seeking to require the federal government to spend dollar-for-dollar the same amount for research that it spent on publicizing the harmful effects of smoking. This was a stance he had staked out since the smoking controversy arose.

Expenditures for both candidates were by present-day standards relatively modest, with Galifianakis outspending Jordan by about $121,000 to $100,000. Approximately a quarter of Nick's campaign chest was contributed by persons of Greek extraction, both in state and out of state, who rallied to the political campaign of one of their own. By comparison, in 1968, when Sam Ervin ran for reelection to the Senate, he collected a few thousand dollars and then returned a good portion of the sum to contributors. The cost of contested campaigns would grow exponentially in the years ahead.

One might have expected the turnout in the May primary to be substantial, not only because of the 26th Amendment, but also because North Carolina had a presidential primary in which a favorite son, former governor Terry Sanford, was a candidate. As the results came in on election night, May 7, 1972, the question was not who would win the primary. Nick took an early lead and gradually increased it. Instead, the question became whether or not he would confound the pundits even further by garnering over 50% of the vote, thereby escaping a second primary. But as the last results came in Galifianakis' percentage was 49.25. Jordan had won 66 of the state's 100 counties, with a percentage of 44.35 but Nick's strength in the urban and suburban areas of the state was overpowering. The race had always been viewed as a two-man contest, a prediction that came true when the two other candidates, J.R. Brown and Eugene Grace, combined for only 6.4% of the vote. Contrary to repeated predictions, Nick had done the impossible. He had toppled an incumbent supported by the party leadership and the party faithful, and he had led the Democratic ticket with a vote total in excess of 375,000.

Those 600 students at Lenoir Community College had predicted the outcome quite well, not only in the Senate race, but in the race for governor and lieutenant governor as well. As the newspapers summed up the results, the state had voted for change, a rejection of the status quo and of those politicians who had long called the shots in the state. The *New York Times* saw the results as an indication of the "'new politics of the young, the black and the anti-establishment." The Democratic establishment's choice for governor had been the lieutenant governor, Pat Taylor, but it was the outsider, Hargrove "Skipper" Bowles, Jr. who won and upset the scenario. And the upstart Galifianakis being the vote leader was hard for the establishment to digest.

Nick at an unusual moment of rest.

Adding support to the claim of a new politics was the beginning of the rise of the Republican Party in the state. The Republican gubernatorial nomination was hotly contested between Jim Gardner and Jim Holshouser. Just over a thousand votes separated the two men, with Gardner in the lead. Only about 170,000 votes were cast in the Republican race, while almost 800,000 were cast in the Democratic vote for governor, demonstrating just how dominant the Democratic Party was in the state. However, there were some ominous signs on the horizon. In the presidential primary, native son Terry Sanford was beaten badly by George Wallace, now running as a Democrat. Wallace seemed to be gaining momentum, not only by winning North Carolina, but also Florida and Tennessee, and finishing second in Wisconsin, Pennsylvania and Indiana. He went on to win Maryland and Michigan, but the day before those votes, he was seriously wounded by an assassin while campaigning in Maryland, and left paralyzed. Many North Carolina voters said that their Wallace vote would be followed by a Nixon vote in November, suggesting continuing Republican strength and showing that the Nixon victory in 1968 was not an aberration.

An interesting sidelight to Wallace's recovery from the assassination attempt concerned the parade of people interested in visiting him in the hospital. When told that Terry Sanford would like to visit, Wallace responded that if North Carolina politicos wanted to send someone, send the guy with the two buttons.

Contributing to the strange political brew in North Carolina was the victory of radio and television commentator Jesse Helms over two rivals in the Republican senatorial primary. His major opponent, James C. Johnson, had argued that Helms' caustic editorials skewering everyone from the popular President Richard M. Nixon to the state governor to teachers at the University of North Carolina at Chapel Hill, and opposing just about all federal policy initiatives of recent years would weaken any chance of a Republican victory in the general election in November. While some saw Helms as a buffoon, others nodded in agreement with his continuing assessment that the country was going to hell. In the primary, Johnson polled less than half of what Helms had. Helms described himself as a reluctant candidate. He certainly was a renegade; one might wonder why a person who opposed just about all federal governmental activity not concerned with fighting communism would want to become part of that government. Could he really hope to change its direction? And could he find being a party man comfortable, after years of lambasting both parties? In the aftermath of his primary victory, he pronounced his success "an invitation by the Republican Party for a bipartisan effort to restore stability to a troubled state and nation."

Actually, Helms had little interest in bipartisanship and its inevitable compromises. Unlike Galifianakis, he had an overall political agenda that looked upon compromise with disdain. He believed that if conservatives were steadfast, no matter what the political cost, they could change the direction of the nation. And what better place to build this movement than from within the bowels of the federal government itself? What Helms brought to a conservativism that long embraced a free enterprise economy, limited government, and anticommunism was a moral fervor that "involved expressing righteous anger to gain attention, deny legitimacy to others, and claim victimhood. It was grounded in a populist religious and racial politics." The 1960s and early 1970s, provided a fertile ground for growth of reactionary politics.

The Helms camp was pleased with the Galifianakis victory, believing that he was much more vulnerable than Jordan would have been. Clearly any Republican victor in the state would have to capture many Democratic voters, along with independents not associated with either major party. No Republican had been elected to any major state or federal office in North Carolina in the twentieth century. Although the incumbent president was popular with voters and likely to win reelection in 1972, would his coattails be long enough to bring along Republican candidates from such strange places as North Carolina?

Before Nick Galifianakis could concentrate on Helms, he had to face the fact that his vote total, though providing an easier victory than anticipated, was not sufficient to avoid a second primary should Jordan decide to call for one. After some delay and some concern among the Democratic political establishment that another primary contest would weaken the party, Jordan apparently became convinced that if he took his opponent more seriously and campaigned vigorously he could emerge victorious. This time, based upon prior experience with second primaries, the positions of the two candidates were reversed, as the odds were now against the incumbent, not the challenger.

On Monday, May 15th the suspense ended as both Democrat Jordan and Republican Holshouser, in their races for the Senate and the governorship respectively, announced their calls for a second primary. It would be held on Saturday, June 3. The fact that the both nominations would be again contested increased chances for a substantial voter turnout.

Jordan had run his first campaign as a frontrunner. This had led him to underestimate Nick as an opponent. A second primary meant that he would have to convince voters, for the first time, that he was the better choice with a proactive campaign that did not fit the 75-year-old man well. While Galifianakis put in long days meeting would-be voters, Jordan was home by nightfall. Also, Jordan could no longer rest on his incumbency. Galifianakis had argued before the first primary vote that Jordan's fourteen-year career as a Senator was matched by Nick's twelve years as a legislator. What was even more helpful for the challenger were his many legislative initiatives, whether in Raleigh or in Washington. He emphasized that Jordan, during his years of service in the Senate, had introduced no major legislation; nor had he gained the seniority that might have put him on important committees. While Nick had gained a spot on the powerful House Appropriations Committee, Jordan dealt with matters of rules and administration that were of little importance to North Carolinians. And even though Jordan sat on the Senate Agriculture Committee, a position that could be used to benefit North Carolina farmers, Galifianakis noted the incumbent had failed to introduce any legislation.

Nick quickly resumed his campaigning, relying, as one political observer said, upon "his highly effective—and less expensive—type of campaigning which is going out to meet the voters face to face and hoping that they will tell the other voters who didn't get to meet him that he is the man they ought to vote for." This old-fashioned person-to-person style "has a strong immediate effect, because if ever a politician had charisma it is Nick the Greek and despite the ethnic background he comes across as a personable 'good old North Carolina boy.'"

The incumbent thought he might get more mileage out of his charge that Nick, in his time-consuming run for the Senate, had neglected his elected duties as a House member—showing up for votes a little over 25% of the time to Jordan's 65%. Apparently, Jordan could not find enough to challenge in regard to his opponent's votes in the House, and therefore concentrated more on the matter of attendance. Galifianakis conceded that his campaign had cut into his House service, but he claimed that during their mutual years of service in Congress his attendance outstripped Jordan's. Nick criticized the incumbent for not responding to the needs of his constituents. He pointed to Jordan's resistance to raising the federal personal federal tax exemption and to the enfranchisement of 18-year olds, along with his votes against medical insurance for the elderly. Nick also repeated the circulating rumor that Jordan, were he to be elected, had no intention of serving a six-year-term, instead stepping down to allow the governor to appoint a successor, a process so common in the state that it seemed to be the norm. Jordan, of course, denied any such intention, but Galifianakis insisted that the voters should assert their authority and end a practice that had, in effect, deprived them of their choice among candidates. Such an assertion not only attacked Jordan, but also the Democratic establishment in the state. Jordan countered by arguing that Nick was not as committed to combating drug abuse as Jordan was, a charge that would survive the primary campaigns. Both men pointed to their efforts to bring projects to North Carolina, sometimes referred to as pork-barrel legislation.

Clearly Nick was a candidate with ideas, a person who was unlikely to be burdened with general understandings of how politics were run in the Old North State. He was a harbinger of a changing South in which the old ways were now being re-inspected.

As the second primary neared a violent incident occurred that momentarily halted the campaign. Jordan, who had been advised to meet voters in the places they congregated, was campaigning at a Raleigh shopping center, North Hills Mall, when a gunman opened fire in the parking lot. The gunman, later identified as Harvey McLeod, had stationed himself between parked cars and randomly shot at people in the lot. Four people were killed and seven injured before McLeod took his own life. One of the injured was Jordan's press secretary, Wes Haden. Jordan was shaken by the experience and rushed to a hospital, but he shortly resumed campaigning, as did his opponent. The attack in Raleigh had not been aimed at Jordan, but the assassinations of the 1960s, along with the Wallace attack, had made politicians wary. Still, fearful of looking weak, when offered protection, the major candidates in North Carolina refused.

When the votes were counted in that second primary, Galifianakis, who had feared that a lighter voter turnout might favor his opponent, had a bigger margin of victory over Jordan than he had in the first primary. The vote was 333,558 to 267, 997. In the Republican primary for governor, Holshouser captured the nomination on his second try. Nick's successor as the Democratic nominee for the House in the 4th District was Ike Andrews, who squeaked out a narrow victory in the second primary over Jyles Coggins. It looked like Nick had made the right choice in giving up the 4th District for a try for a Senate seat.

In the past, a victory in the Democratic primary meant a victory in November's general election. However, as Nick's success illustrated, politics in North Carolina were in a state of flux. Remember Wallace's victory over favorite son Sanford in May, and the view of many that those votes would turn into votes for a second term for President Nixon in November? That prediction would only gain strength when the Democratic Convention produced its candidate, the liberal from South Dakota, three-term Senator George McGovern, who had not even been on the North Carolina presidential primary ballot. What had happened since the Nixon victory in 1968 was the reconfiguration of the Democratic Party. The 1972 party convention was much more fully representative of the rank and file of the party, with substantial increases in the presence of women, minorities, and the young, much to the displeasure of the party's old guard. As the nation sought respite from the turmoil of the 60s and early 70s, the electorate moved in a more politically conservative direction. Vice-President Spiro Agnew's harangues against radicals and liberals became increasingly appealing.

As a further illustration of the changing political scene, one need look no further than the Republican opponent Nick would have to defeat in November—Jesse Helms. Until 1970, Helms had been a Democrat. In the Republican primary, Helms had defeated a member of the Party's old guard, who had insisted that Jesse's strongly expressed public views about practically everything doomed any chance of political success. Nick had been criticized for his moderation, his unwillingness to take strong positions that might alienate certain voters. Certainly Jesse Helms suffered from no such liability.

With his second primary election victory behind him, Nick could now turn to his Republican opponent. While some political observers did not take Helms' candidacy seriously, Galifianakis, after years of experience with closely contested elections, would not be overconfident.

INTERLUDE 11

Working and Playing with Presidents

During Galifianakis' three terms in Congress, he served under two different presidents and was a colleague of two fellow representatives who would come to serve in the nation's highest office.

In his first term, at a meeting with President Lyndon Johnson and a dozen other newly elected Democratic congressmen, Galifianakis must have impressed the president, for he was asked to stay behind as the others left. Nick said he had come with David Pryor, a representative from Arkansas, and the president said David could stay also. Mint julips were served, and Johnson reminisced about his days as a school teacher and talked about his beautiful and wealthy wife, Lady Bird. He also asked after two important black leaders in Durham, John Wheeler, the president of Mechanics and Farmers Bank, and Asa Spaulding, president of the North Carolina Mutual Life Insurance Company. Galifianakis was surprised that the president was familiar with them and remarked that both men seemed to be in good health.

Despite the warm initial encounter, Nick's outspoken opposition to the war in Vietnam did not result in any close relationship with the White House during his first term. The White House had lobbied for Galifianakis' vote on the Fair Housing Act of 1968. Nick realized that a vote for the act would not play well with North Carolinians, but he appeared ready to cast it. Before that vote was called for, he received a call from the White House saying that his vote was not needed and that it was more important that he be reelected than that he cast an unpopular vote. The actual vote in the House was 326 to 93 in favor of the Act.

Nick found his relationship with the White House improving after the election of Richard Nixon in 1968. President Nixon felt a bond with Nick since they were both graduates of the School of Law at Duke University. The president actually came to the floor of the House to personally greet the fellow law graduate. William "Fishbait" Miller, the House Doorkeeper remarked that such a presidential greeting was unprecedented. Socially, this kinship resulted in abundant invitations to White House dinners. Congressmen, especially relative newcomers, were rarely invited to sit-down dinners. Invitations to receptions were relatively common; invitations to dinner were not. Generally, when Louise Galifianakis was available in Washington, she refused to go to the White House for dinner because of her dislike of the president. Nick tried to convince her that a refusal showed disrespect for the presidency, something which she denied. When once she said she would go, she also said she needed a proper dress. When Nick was presented with the bill of $1000, he wondered how a dress could cost so much. He got the message and decided not to urge his wife to accept any more Nixon dinner invitations.

Galifianakis' relationship with Gerald Ford began as a colleague in the House of Representatives. Nick's first contact with Ford came on the House floor when the Michigan representative presented the freshman congressman with five crisp hundred dollar bills. This was a gift from one of Ford's campaign advisors who was pleased that a person of Greek extraction had been elected to Congress. The gift came with the proviso that it not be revealed until Ford had died. Galifianakis cited Thomas Jefferson's rules that governed the House, stipulating that money not be passed on the House floor. Ford responded that was the reason for the proviso. Subsequently, the man who would become president upon the resignation of Richard Nixon often consulted Nick in regard to certain pieces of proposed legislation. In most cases, Galifianakis pledged his support. However, when Ford sought support for a resolution to impeach Supreme Court Justice William O. Douglas, Nick demurred, saying that Douglas was one of his heroes.

During Nick's years in Congress he also served with George H. W. Bush, who considered himself quite an accomplished racquetball player. Bush often played with Bob Mathias, another congressman, best known for winning Olympic gold in the decathlon. One day Mathias, who had a commitment that conflicted with his scheduled match with Bush, asked Galifianakis to fill in. Nick sought to demur on the basis that he was not that skilled at the game, but he eventually agreed. With a racket that had seen better days and a makeshift outfit that included black tennis shoes that he bought at a Piggly Wiggly, Nick showed up for the game. In a closely contested match, Galifianakis emerged victorious. The gym master was so delighted with Nick's victory that he kept the match's score posted until Bush complained. In response, the gym master had a brass plaque made commemorating the match's outcome, which he displayed on the wall.

Nick with Telly Savalas. In addition to presidents, Nick often crossed paths with famous actors and leaders in other fields.

CHAPTER XII

Seeking a Senate Seat in a Perfect Storm of State and National Politics, 1972

The historical importance of the 1972 race for the Senate seat was obvious even as it was being run. More than a contest between Galifianakis and Helms or between a Democrat and a Republican, it was a contest to determine whether North Carolinians were ready to embrace the future or destined to remain burdened by the past. Oddly, Helms, the candidate of the past, would embrace the campaign tools of the future and Galifianakis, the candidate of the future, would employ the methods of the past.

Race had brought the solid Democratic South into being following the Civil War, and race was now bringing about the party's demise. Cracks were visible as early as 1948 when President Harry Truman, thrust into the office upon the death of Franklin D. Roosevelt, ran for reelection. His civil rights stance alienated many North Carolinians, but he still won the state's electoral vote. Republican Dwight David Eisenhower came close to the prize in his reelection bid in 1956, but the Old North State's citizens stood behind the Democratic candidate through Lyndon Baines Johnson's election in 1964.

In 1968, Johnson's vice-president, Democrat Hubert Humphrey, an early and strong supporter of civil rights legislation, ran third in the presidential vote in North Carolina, beaten by both Republican Richard Nixon and the American Independent Party candidate George Wallace, a dedicated racist. When Nixon won the state's electoral vote, it was clear that a Republican Party that had turned lily-white in the early twentieth century was on the rise. This new version of the party was a far cry from the party of Lincoln. Shedding its early history, the Republican Party became most attractive to those Southern whites who were increasingly convinced that gains for blacks meant losses for whites, especially after the Civil Rights Act of 1964.

The traditional Southern Democrats were also diluted by the internal migration of the U.S. population from north to south. The Piedmont area, Nick's former stronghold and the center of substantial economic activity, saw the greatest population growth. The new arrivals had no historical ties to the Democratic Party. They were the political center, a largely white, middle-class population, attracted by the economic planks in the Republican Party's platform. North Carolina's reputation for progressive views not only on economic matters but also on race would be tested in this new environment, partly because that reputation had been built on a foundation of black deference that would not survive the civil rights movement.

Perhaps even more important than migration as a portent of the future was George Wallace's appeal to North Carolina white voters. Polls in 1968 revealed that only 17% of whites favored racially integrated neighborhoods and only 23% favored integrated schools. Observers did not need polls to conclude that white North Carolinians resented the rise of black power and the movement toward racial equality. Wallace had been praised by Jesse Helms for his opposition to the civil rights movement. Regarding that part of the civil rights movement led by Dr. Martin Luther King, Jr., Helms said: "It is about as nonviolent as the Marines landing on Iwo Jima, and it is a 'movement' only in the sense that mob action is moving and spreading throughout the land." Wallace tapped into such feelings.

Within this turbulent environment, Nick Galifianakis would be running the hardest race of his life under rules that were changing every day. For the time being, however, Nick's old-fashioned politics seemed adequate to the immediate task before him. Had he not toppled an incumbent? Had he not traveled extensively throughout the state so that all North Carolinians knew who he was, whether they could spell his name or not? Furthermore, he would start with clear frontrunner status—almost three quarters of the state voters were registered Democrats, and no Republican had been elected to the Senate from North Carolina in the twentieth century.

But, coupled with the fact that a Democratic Party nomination might no longer be a guarantee of success in the general election, the nature of political campaigning was changing quickly. John F. Kennedy in 1960 demonstrated what an ally television could be, and Lyndon B. Johnson used television ads to complete the destruction of Barry Goldwater, his Republican opponent in 1964. Politics had already become professionalized, but now it was a matter of assembling experts to craft not only the candidate's image, but also that of his opponent. Successful campaigns would now rely upon relatively expensive media campaigns to reach audiences. In part for this reason, campaigns of the future would require previously unheard of amounts of money.

From the outset, it was a strange political battle for "one of the most ethnically homogeneous states in the country." It pitted a Greek-American, who had tapped liberal sentiment in the Piedmont area by successfully arguing for a future quite different from the past, against an opinionated conservative radio and television commentator. Helms, along with many people in the state, wanted to preserve as much of that past as was possible. One candidate summoned up visions of the future, the other extolled a vanishing past. Neither candidate was thoroughly embraced by his party or enthusiastically supported by the party's other candidates for political office. The voters would have to decide which man better symbolized where the state was in 1972. Either way, change was in the offing.

Jesse Helms, as a television editorialist, had regularly mocked politicians, Nick included. Now in contemplating the race ahead, Helms made much of his characterization of Galifianakis as not being "one of us." Its very ambiguity made the phrase all the more attractive, for clearly a deep divide separated the two candidates. Just who were "us?" Was the Greek Orthodox faith less Christian than the Baptist variety? Was the "us" defined by those who agreed with Helms' diatribes; if so, how large was that following? Although both men were native-born North Carolinians, Nick's ties with the state began when his Greek father settled in North Carolina in 1919. Helms, on the other hand, could trace his English and Scots-Irish ancestry back to the mid-18th century.

Helms was born in 1921 in Monroe, about twenty-five miles east of Charlotte, the state's largest city. Raised in the conservative Southern Baptist tradition, Helms grew up in a rigidly racially-segregated society. From his perspective, it was a society that suited and satisfied both races. This assumption led him to view the civil rights movement as one that was forced upon the South by outsiders. Helms' interest in journalism was sparked in high school, and, as an adult, he obtained a position at the *Raleigh Times*, to which he returned after his service in World War II as a navy recruiter. His prose was colorful and accessible, and as a re-cruiter he had learned something about persuading others. Furthermore, he had begun exploring the advantages of radio broadcasting over print. Helms believed that print was less effective as an advertising medium, and the advantage of broadcasting was further confirmed when television arrived. Over the next twenty-some years he would serve as a radio broadcaster, congressional aide, editor of the *Tarheel Banker*, lobbyist for the banking industry, and television executive and commentator. Helms decried the actions of the federal government, and saw the shift of politics to the left pushing the country into socialism and destroying the individual initiative that had made the country great. His anti-communism was a broad umbrella under which he justified his attacks on liberals.

His position as a television commentator on WRAL from 1960 to 1972 gave him a forum to broadcast his views. He gained a great following in the eastern part of the state, where his *Viewpoint* broadcasts were fed and where his newspaper columns found eager readers. Although considered no less than the incarnation of the devil by many faculty and students at the University of North Carolina in Chapel Hill, a bastion of Southern liberalism, Jesse was applauded elsewhere for "telling it like it is." One commentator said that Helms' "devoutly right-wing, discreetly segregationist" editorials were "much admired in rural, conservative eastern North Carolina." Another observer, impressed with Helms' influence in the area, said "It's been like the voice of God down in these parts." In fact, in his opposition to a state zoo, Helms said the state already had the makings of one, and that all that was needed to complete it was the erection of a fence around the institution in Chapel Hill.

The only elected office Helms had held consisted of two terms as a city councilman in Raleigh from 1957 to 1961. Often outvoted by the majority because of his decisions against spending money, he decided not to seek a third term. However, he did eye a bid for the state senate. The incumbent in 1961, John Jordan, Jr., had told Jesse that he would not run again, but Governor Terry Sanford convinced Jordan to change his mind, leaving Helms resentful. Undoubtedly Helms was delighted when, in 1972, George Wallace defeated Sanford in the state's first presidential primary.

In addition to holding public office, albeit briefly, Helms worked behind the scenes on campaigns. Many considered the nastiest political race in the history of the state to be the 1950 Democratic primary between incumbent Frank Porter Graham, the former University of North Carolina president, and challenger Willis Smith, a Raleigh attorney. Dr. Frank, as he was called, was a highly regarded and gentle man, but one who took positions on unions and on racial matters that antagonized conservatives. When that fact was combined with Graham's connection with liberal groups that often were seen as friendly to communists, the Smith forces launched a vicious attack on the much loved incumbent. Helms said he, too, loved Graham but disagreed with him politically.

Although Helms denied that he played any role in the viciousness of the campaign, his recollection was challenged by others. Certainly he played a prominent role in support of Smith, and the negative campaign style would live on in subsequent elections in both North Carolina and the nation. It springs from the essential premise that anybody would be better than the attacked candidate. From the start, the Smith supporters were aggressive, pointing to their opponent's association with communists, his vigorous support for the demands of labor, and his failure to defend white supremacy. Smith's ads pictured a mixing of the races and suggested that was what Graham wanted. Furthermore, Smith's campaign sent out ads, purportedly from the National Association for the Advancement of Colored People (NAACP), commending the incumbent on all he had done for black people in North Carolina. Yet, with all this negativity, Graham won by 53,000 votes. However, his total was slightly less than 49%, giving Smith the opportunity to call for a second primary. Smith was in favor of accepting the outcome; he was tired of campaigning. His resistance was overcome when Jesse Helms and the owner of the radio station, WRAL, under the banner of "Citizens Committee for Willis Smith" financed 30-second radio spots, during three hours of recorded music, that urged the challenger's supporters to go to Smith's home to urge him to call for a second primary. About 400 people showed up, enough to convince Smith to call for that second vote.

In the nineteen days until the second election, the Smith forces attacked Graham's support of big federal government, his conciliatory racial attitude, and his failure to take a strong stand in the fight against communism. The campaign sought to join anti-communism with the racial issue. With words and pictures, it conjured up what many North Carolinians found horrifying—an integrated society. In the end, the campaign worked, and a larger than expected turnout gave Smith the victory by nearly 20,000 votes. Helms left his job as news director of radio WRAL and served as Smith's congressional aide for twenty months from January 1952 to September 1953.

Clearly the Republican Party had been growing in the South, and because it was a relatively new force in Southern politics it could accommodate recent converts, such as Jesse Helms. Only eight years earlier, Democrat Strom Thurmond, South Carolina's senator, found a new home in the Republican Party. Perhaps Helms could bring his supporters in Eastern North Carolina to his new party. Listeners there felt that the broadcaster captured their own frustration with the recent course of events. What Helms brought to such views was a colorful, sarcastic way of expressing them, often making particular individuals or measures the target of his commentaries. Despite the clear gains made in civil rights throughout the country, racism continued to pervade much of the North Carolina population and indeed the entire South. In the early seventies the nation had committed itself to affirmative action and although the Supreme Court had yet to square it with the Constitution, considerable segments of the American population felt that such preferences constituted reverse discrimination. Helms tapped into this sentiment and exploited an orneriness that many observers said characterized North Carolina voters.

Winning the California primary in June seemed to assure liberal Senator George McGovern of the Democratic nomination for president, but that was not secured until the Democrats met in Miami in mid-July. The McGovern candidacy was a godsend for Helms, who consistently linked his opponent, Nick Galifianakis, to the Democratic presidential candidate. Calling his campaign a crusade with a message for Washington, Helms said "that the people of North Carolina are totally unwilling to accept any longer a U. S. Senate too timid to stand up to the McGoverns and all other apostles of Socialism." The fact that McGovern won the nomination when so many traditional Democratic leaders and groups opposed him made party unification impossible. Nick answered by saying he did not care which presidential candidate North Carolinians selected.

Helms' earlier criticism of President Richard M. Nixon now disappeared as Helms sought to take advantage of the president's strong lead in the polls. The television editorialist turned politician now avoided all criticism of the president and basked in the glow of Nixon's increasing popularity.

Although Governor Bob Scott, as a loyal Democrat, endorsed McGovern, he had nothing to lose. Nick Galifianakis, however, did. McGovern's pronounced liberalism did not resonate with many North Carolinians. Nick's record in the House did reveal some endorsement of liberal policies, and Helms was quick to pounce on this part of his voting record, contending that McGovern and Galifianakis were two peas in the same pod. When members of the Kiwanis Club in Dunn indicated their preference in September Galifianakis got 22% to Helms' 78%. Nixon got almost 93%, while McGovern could not quite get 4%. The *Carolina Financial Times*' readers responded similarly with 89% for Nixon and 60% for Helms. For Galifianakis, the clear front-runner, to do so very poorly, even in such unscientific polls, was not good news.

Helms picked up one of Jordan's campaign issues when he called attention to his opponent's absence when the House of Representatives voted on certain pieces of drug legislation. The advertisement supposedly placed by doctors in support of Helms' candidacy was titled "Where Was Nick?" It suggested that Galifianakis' absence indicated that he did not place drug abuse high on his agenda of concerns. It had been designed to capitalize on popular concern about the issue. Helms' campaign manager, Tom Ellis, accused Galifianakis of waging a war on drugs through press releases and attaching himself to legislation proposed by others, saying "He jumps on bills the way a caboose jumps on a train." Nick sought to set the record straight by listing the various bills he had sponsored in the House. Furthermore, he added, three of the laws the ad embraced had no substantial opposition, and the one that did had nothing to do with drug abuse.

When the Helms campaign conceded that it in fact had paid for the ad, numerous letters and editorials in various North Carolina newspapers criticized the Helms campaign for its attempt to mislead voters. The *Winston-Salem Journal* was especially incensed by the ad. Noting that Helms had made a career of exposing "dupes," the editorialist continued: "Preparing such an ad and then failing to identify it as part of the Helms campaign are actions that speak for themselves, and we wouldn't pursue the incident if Helms himself were not so pious about the shortcomings of others." Then the writer, noting that many newspapers ran the ad without seeking and printing its attribution, concluded that perhaps Helms was right in assuming "that the newspaper business would be full of" such dupes. Criticism of the attack on Galifianakis was so widespread that Helms had to deny that he had seen the ad before its publication and promise that henceforth he would personally approve any campaign ad before it made its way into print. Such backtracking was unusual for Helms, who almost never changed course as a result of criticism.

Republican Senators Barry Goldwater and Strom Thurmond came to North Carolina to aid Helms' campaign. Also appearing to lend support to Helms' campaign was Vice-President Spiro Agnew, who ignored the Greek heritage he shared with Galifianakis and endorsed the former broadcaster. Agnew's speech in Winston-Salem was largely a defense of Nixon's foreign policy. Whether the vice-president knew it or not, Helms had been a consistent critic of the president's foreign policy. Perhaps the irony was lost in the politics of the situation.

Galifianakis had the support of Wilbur Mills of Arkansas, chairman of the powerful House Ways and Means Committee, who campaigned for Nick, and Senator Sam Ervin, Jr., who was now vigorous in his support for the man who had defeated Jordan. (All pictured below along with Mike Mansfield.)

North Carolina's senior senator noted that should a Republican Senate emerge from the general election in 1972, he would be stripped of four committee chairmanships and North Carolina would lose a forceful voice. Ervin said that the Republican Party's Southern strategy was harmful to Southern interests. Those interests, he continued, are best protected by insuring the majority position of the Democratic Party in the Senate, "the remaining citadel of Southern strength and influence in national politics."

That Republican strategy sought to tap into a Southern resentment over the civil rights movement. On the matter of race, the Raleigh *News & Observer* said "It is a matter of commonplace conversation, not whispers, that he [Helms] has been the most notable antagonist of Negro rights in the last 10 years in North Carolina." When North Carolina voters were asked to list the important issues in the coming election, Vietnam was subordinated to crime, poverty and busing, all of which implicated race. The capital city's paper said that race was the "dirty little secret that is neither little nor a secret, but central to current politics."

Helms said his top priority was to help bring about "a spiritual rebirth" in the country, thus giving an early voice to the social conservatives who would assume increasing importance in the Republican Party over the decades. Taking aim on what he called the socialistic welfare state, the power of federal judges, and finally the "tragic folly of federal control of education," he asserted that his views have not and would not change. He said the present contest could be best characterized as a choice between a "conservative" and a "spender," leaving no doubt as to which of the two he was. Despite Helms' denial, he did moderate some of the strong views he had uttered as a broadcaster. For instance, in 1970 he said social security benefits were "nothing more than doles and handouts distributed on a politically oriented schedule." In 1972, as a candidate, he said the system was needed and that he had never attacked the concept, only its implementation.

Nick was an experienced legislator and he had given considerable thought to how Congress might become a more effective body, while Helms took issue with just about all federal programs except those that provided for national defense. Galifianakis proposed a four-year term for House members, in part to provide more stability in Congress so that it could pay more attention to the nation's fiscal business. He felt that appropriations were handled in a haphazard way by the legislative branch in large part because of the two-year term for House members.

Helms sought to blame Nick for increases in crime and inflation, adding that the congressman was soft on drug control, less than patriotic in his lack of support for the Vietnam War, and finally somehow responsible for the civil rights movement. In addition to his continuing support for the Vietnam War effort, the broadcaster wanted less federal government spending and less interference in state matters and both tax and welfare reform.

In the midst of this battling, the Republican challenger did concede, in an unusual moment of introspection, that he lacked charisma. What Helms did to make up for his lack of charisma was create a self-image that set him apart from politics. He would "tell it like it was," whether he was the editorialist on WRAL or whether he was the people's choice to represent them in the Senate. Often implicitly but sometimes directly, Nick was criticized for his political sense—a willingness to compromise one's views, either for electoral success or, more often, to accommodate differences and arrive at a real solution to a problem.

At any rate, the voters would decide whether running for political office while criticizing politics and denying that one was a politician could trump charisma. The *Charlotte News* concluded that both political parties were not entirely happy with their senatorial candidates. Some Democrats lamented that Galifianakis was not cut from the same cloth as Sam Ervin, Jr., and some Republicans complained that Helms' views were too extreme to represent the views of North Carolina Republicans.

Nick continued to rely on his personal style of campaigning and the news attention he could attract, convinced that it could fill the gap that a shortage of money left. Helms grasped the future of political campaigning in the country, as he said: "You can shake all the hands you want, but nothing will get you better known than exposure through the media." To illustrate the campaign differences, Helms planned to all but eliminate personal appearances in the last few days before the election, content that his political ads were sufficient to do the job. Galifianakis, on the other hand, would continue to schedule news conferences and seek hands to shake until time ran out. Nick believed that there was no substitute for personal contact, saying that it was "real," while advertising was "artificial." He never doubted his ability to win voters to his side, but the question of whether he could personally engage enough voters to outpoll an opponent skillfully using the media still remained.

In a special effort to appeal to Democrats, knowing that he could only be elected if Democrats deserted their party's candidate, Helms used pictures and comments of prominent state Democrats that had been taken or written years earlier to suggest their support of his candidacy. Their protest led Helms to back away from such tactics. Galifianakis, on the other hand, had to keep Democrats faithful to their party, especially those voters in the more rural eastern part of the state who found Helms attractive. Nick noted that the television commentator in some thirty instances had railed against agricultural price supports, obviously an important issue to Eastern North Carolina's farmers. Galifianakis, however, would find, as many politicians have before and since, that American voters did not always vote their economic self-interest.

John E. Semonche

INTERLUDE 12

Louise Galifianakis

When Nick married Lou he knew they shared the same core beliefs about people and the world. She was a kindred political soul, although at times a more fervent Democrat and anti-Republican than her husband. What he did not know was the latent talent she possessed as a campaigner.

Louise Galifianakis hard at work and in her element.

Nick's campaigns for federal office were family affairs that often pressed Nick's mother and his brothers into service, but, with the exception of the candidate himself, no one outdid Lou. During the Senate run in 1972 she matched her husband's 15-16 hour days on the campaign trail. Often she would say: "I'd rather make a speech than a bed." In the past, she said, she would have had difficulty walking into a roomful of strangers and opening her mouth. No more. Nick and Lou did not campaign together; separately they could reach more people. When Nick would miss scheduled gatherings, most often because he had to be in Washington, she substituted for him. And Nick was both disappointed and pleased when a request for an appearance came in and it was for Lou and not him.

Lou enjoyed speaking to the issues and tended, as much as possible, to avoid tea parties or other women-only affairs. While Nick avoided talking about his opponent, Jesse Helms, Lou did not hesitate to condemn his negative campaigning and explain how the broadcaster compared with her husband. While Nick was positive and forward looking, she would say Jesse was negative and fearful of the future. And while Nick had six years of experience working in Congress, Jesse had four years on the Raleigh City Council. She could not understand why anyone would puzzle over the choice.

Although Lou did not consider herself an argumentative feminist, she did believe that women should have equal rights under the law. In the political arena with which she had become familiar, women did far more of the work than was generally recognized, despite their relative absence from political office. As evidence, she pointed to Margaret Sugg, who, as Nick's administrative assistant, ran both the office and the congressman himself.

With the Senate campaign was underway Nick was confronted with a vote in the House of Representatives on sending the Equal Rights Amendment to the states for ratification. Senator Sam Ervin approached Nick with the request that he join the rest of the North Carolina congressional delegation and make the vote against the proposed amendment unanimous. Ervin argued that what women really wanted was not the same rights as men but simply courteous behavior. By way of explanation for why he could not join Ervin, Nick responded: "Senator Sam, you forget who I married." Senator Sam remembered Louise and argued no more.

Louise with children, Jon Mark, Katherine. and Stephanie.

238

CHAPTER XIII

Galifianakis v. Helms:
The Storm Intensifies in a Changing South, 1972

With the coming of fall, Nick was still securely ahead in the race. In fact, in their syndicated column that appeared in The *Washington Post* on September 20, Rowland Evans and Robert Novak highlighted the North Carolina race for the purpose of demonstrating just how short Nixon's coattails seemed to be. Galifianakis was ahead in the polls by 52% to 40%. Noting that in the past Helms had called Nixon a communist appeaser but was now holding his tongue, the columnists concluded that the former broadcaster was still identified by his "hard-right ideological manifestos" that made him "an unreconstructed conservative in a moderate state." Also working against the Helms' candidacy, they said, was the fact that one could not vote a straight party ticket in North Carolina, there being three separate ballots: one for president, another for statewide candidates, and the third for local candidates. Evans and Novak also commended Nick on his ability to stride the path of moderation, saying "in Galifianakis Helms confronts a politician of subtle skills who, despite his reputation as left of center, has compiled a voting average hardly displeasing to the moderate right." Thus protecting "his flank on the right, with strong support from farmers and small-town merchants," Nick, they continued, has placated the left with his "early dovish position on immediate withdrawal from the Vietnam war." With no big bounce from Nixon's five to one lead over McGovern, the columnists concluded, Helms could only win by pulling "himself up by his own bootstraps," and that, they said, "seems beyond his capacity." The *Shelby Daily Star* agreed, expressing surprise that Helms now claimed that Nixon needed him in the Senate. Suggesting that "political expediency had indeed created a Helms credibility gap," the *Star* told its readers to expect Helms, should he be elected, to oppose "practically every program . . . the president proposes."

Other writers, however, noticed that the Republicans needed only five more seats to take control in the Senate and were not ready to conclude that Nixon had no coattails. The *Washington Post* seemed to be especially intrigued by the North Carolina race. One of its reporters, Jonathan Yardley, said that the political neophyte Helms needed Nixon's help to have a chance of winning, despite the "built-in constituency" that his radio and television broadcasts had garnered. Helms would eventually get that help, as the White House seemed to be focusing its attention on this particular Senate race. While in 1968 Nixon was not able to share his popularity with other candidates, that popularity in both the South and the nation had grown considerably in four years. Yardley further wrote that with his slogan of "He's not one of us," Helms suggested that Galifianakis, a native North Carolinian, was a foreigner, that his religion, Greek Orthodox, was suspect, and that the candidate's so-called moderation was a façade behind which hid a McGovern liberal. The reporter assessed Helms' chances as good with that approach, calculating a Republican base of about 45% of the vote, which meant that the broadcaster would need less than 200,000 disgruntled or alienated Democrats to cast their votes for him. This analysis did not mean the reporter favored Helms. Compared to Helms, Yardley wrote that Galifianakis was no less than a statesman.

Another *Washington Post* reporter, William Chapman,

called the North Carolina race "one of the roughest political slugfests North Carolina has seen since the late Frank Graham was red-baited out of a Senate seat in 1950." As Helms held his tongue about his differences with the Nixon administration, he repeatedly associated Galifianakis with the unpopular Democratic presidential candidate McGovern. Both men, Helms said, "voted similarly to 'cut and run' out of Vietnam and to support welfare 'giveaways.'" Nick argued that he supported more of Nixon's initiatives than had the broadcaster. When confronted with his labeling of Nixon as a communist appeaser, Helms said he had simply used "literary license."

The large lead that Nick had held as late as the first of October was beginning to shrink. To take advantage, Helms' campaign planned a series of television commercials emphasizing that the president needed a Republican Senate, and that the election of Helms would help achieve this goal. Although some of Helms' attacks on Nick backfired, they were more often than not effective. Even the always exuberant Nick was feeling the strain, and Senator Ervin complained that Democrats were not enthusiastically supporting their own candidates. In fact, some prominent Democrats, such as J. Melville Broughton, Jr, former chairmen of the North Carolina Democratic Party, and Joe Hunt, the campaign manager for former governor Dan Moore, publicly supported Helms.

Helms' relentless media campaign surged in the last month before the election, merging the candidacies of McGovern and Galifianakis, contending that they were cut from the same liberal cloth. Full page newspaper ads on October 4th proclaimed "McGovernGalifianakis—one and the same." Continually, Nick was on the defensive, trying to counter the smears and distortions of the ads. There was little he could do, though, to counter the "Helms is one of us and the other guy is not" approach. Despite presenting evidence of Helms' strong and unmodified criticisms of a president that he now so proudly embraced, Nick could not check the erosion of his earlier lead. When Helms' supporters co-signed a $100,000 bank loan late in the campaign, the advertisements it financed continued to chip away at Nick's lead. With such ads filling the airwaves, Nick started to accuse his opponent of running a "smear-type campaign" in violation of "the traditions of politics in North Carolina."

A cartoon joining Galifianakis with McGovern.

On the defensive, Galifianakis tried to separate Helms from his new-found friend, President Nixon. In his past WRAL editorials Helms had criticized Nixon's economic policies as "futile, reckless, and almost laughable." While Helms was merging Galifianakis with McGovern, Nick was desperately seeking to undo the merger of Nixon with Helms. His campaign was dissecting those old WRAL editorials. What they revealed was Helms' constant criticism of Nixon's foreign policy as "selling out to the Communists." The Republican senatorial candidate, Nick said, was now running away from the opinions he had expressed as a television commentator. This heavier emphasis on Helms' changed views may have come too late to slow Helms' momentum. The former broadcaster, of course, denied any political adjustment, saying that critics mistook the details he was now giving as changes in his views. When Helms claimed that his views were consistent and clear, Galifianakis detailed numerous instances where this claim just did not hold up. Nixon's attempt to improve relations with the Soviet Union and China, rural electrification, Medicare, agricultural price supports, social security, and the vote for 18 year-olds were all opposed by Helms; now he seemed to be relinquishing ownership of these views. Nick just could not believe that North Carolinians would send a senator to Washington who wanted to enshrine the status quo and "obstruct new ideas and new hope."

Galifianakis' failure to get much mileage out of Helms' Nixon-bashing editorials stemmed both from the congressman being placed on the defensive and from the fact the vast majority of the 2,732 *Viewpoints* concerned attacks on liberal policies, the civil rights movement and especially the written press. Perhaps surprising is the fact that Helms, a media person, made a medium—the written press—a main target. Of course, the major dailies in the state were sharp critics of Helms, none more than the Raleigh *News & Observer*.

Nick tried to counter the image engineered by the Helms' campaign—that Galifianakis was a liberal, no different than the Democratic Party's standard bearer, George McGovern. As his record showed, Nick satisfied neither liberals nor conservatives, and he prided himself on the fact that he could not be pigeon-holed. When Ralph Nader's Congress Project expressed frustration at not being able to characterize Nick, the congressman was delighted, for it only reinforced the image he wanted to project. As he said, "I want to be a senator, not an unelected purist." Despite overwhelming evidence that Nick's political position could best be described as moderate, Helms' characterization of his opponent as a liberal was an effective attack. Many North Carolina voters held liberals responsible for all that was wrong in America. That wrong course included a disrespect for law and order, the ready availability of sexually explicit material, the rejection of traditional family values, the secular society that barred religion from the public schools, and the favoritism afforded blacks.

The campaigns traded barbs about how they were financed. Nick accused Helms of a campaign "built around dollars, not people." Tom Ellis, Helms' campaign manager, countered that Nick was "running with huge amounts of money from out-of-state, from union bosses, and from special interest groups." Nick's campaign manager, Russell Walker, responded that his rival was simply trying to obscure the fact that Helms' campaign had been dominated by "huge special interests."

In the final analysis, what Helms had that Galifianakis lacked was money, which was increasingly becoming the power behind political success. During a six-week period from September 1, 1972 to mid-October, Helms had placed more than 1500 ads in 230 newspapers to Nick's single ad in one paper. He had more than twice as many television spots—his purchase of television ads late in the campaign was limited only because stations had run out of time to sell. Overall, from the first of September into late October, Helms outspent Galifianakis $265,000 to $74,000. From the first of the year, the totals were $436,135 and $268,673 respectively.

As polls showed the gap between the candidates narrowing, Helms received more attention and more money. The Republican Boosters Club contributed $40,000 and the Republican Senatorial Campaign Committee $30,000. The White House authorized the use of Nixon's support of Helms on billboards, the only race in the country where that was allowed.

Sharing the *Washington Post's* interest in the North Carolina senatorial race, Marjorie Hunter made sure *New York Times* readers knew that the White House had poured both money and resources into the Helms campaign. Hunter also noted that Nick's victory over Jordan in the primaries had alienated some prominent Democrats who now were campaigning for Helms. She concluded, as had others, that the lead that Nick had was now gone and the race had become too close to call.

The heavy spending illustrated how one campaign was largely focused on media exposure, and the other on personal contact. Helms, with his media experience, realized that a candidate could get considerably more mileage out of money spent on advertising than that spent in other ways. Also, an ad-based campaign better suited a personality that did not relish the kind of personal contact that was a hall-mark of Nick's political success.

Nick campaigning with Senator Sam Ervin, Sophis, Louise and Nick's brother, Harry.

With the election approaching, Howard Covington, a *Charlotte Observer* reporter, interviewed the candidates. Helms asserted his belief in states' rights, freedom of choice in the public schools, and the need to bring some "sanity" to public finance by reducing the nation's huge debt. Nick on the other hand was less specific, stressing his energy and reasserting his belief that "public office is a public trust." Covington concluded that a vote for Helms would be a repudiation of "North Carolina's long-standing reputation for political moderation and Southern leadership." Harkening back to 1950 when Willis Smith, with help from a young Jesse Helms, ran a scurrilous Democratic primary campaign accusing Frank Porter Graham of favoring communism and racial mixing, the reporter accused Helms of opposing "much of the forward movement of this state and the region over the past 12 years." Among the broadcaster's targets were desegregation, Medicare, welfare reform, electric co-ops, public housing, and prison reform. Organizations he condemned included the League of Women Voters, the United Nations, and the Peace Corps.

On the other hand, Covington continued, Nick in his three terms in the House "contributed to commonsense progress" with a record that truly reflected the moderate views that were characteristic of the state's people. Galifianakis had cast one of only two North Carolina votes for extending the Civil Rights Commission, and he was the first member of the delegation to hire a black aide. The *Observer* also noted what it considered a special and valuable trait in the Congressman: his advocacy "of a vigilant Congress against the encroaching power of the White House."

Paul Clancy of the *Charlotte Observer* noted in late October that Helms had continued to narrow the gap between himself and Nick. The reporter wrote that "heavy advertising and frequent slashing attacks against his [Galifianakis'] character and record" were hurting the front-runner. Helms was incessantly questioning Nick's patriotism by stressing the Congressman's opposition to the war in Vietnam. Furthermore, the Helms' campaign was saturating evening television broadcasting with ads claiming "Nixon needs him." To counter the strategy, Senator Ervin, increasingly disturbed by defections, said that "Democrats who don't look after their own kind are worse than infidels."

Both Charlotte newspapers endorsed Nick. The *Observer* concluded that Galifianakis had established a legislative record based on "political thinking that has been prevalent in the state in recent years," while Helms' views were "certain to take the state in the opposite direction." The *Charlotte News* said that Nick had solid legislative experience and stood "in the broad middle ground with most of the state's citizens," while Helms' "ultra-conservative editorial positions" were just not those of a majority of North Carolinians.

A poll taken by the *Charlotte News* in Mecklenburg County, viewed as one of Galifianakis' strongholds, revealed that in the month from October 3 to November 3, the 51%-28% edge for Nick had been reversed. Helms now had the edge at 48% to 38% with the remainder undecided. Voters were reminded by the newspaper that, unlike many political contests they covered, the one between Nick and Jesse was one of stark contrasts.

Nixon made a late visit to North Carolina on November 4, now fairly sure that the Republicans would pick up the seat. Private polls by both candidates revealed the dramatic change. Nick, however, continued to believe that the polls were wrong. Befuddled by the political change taking place, Nick said of those voters in the east: "Those people have always voted Democratic and if they vote for Nixon this round, they'll do penance by switching to vote for me."

On the eve of the election, a prominent odds-maker, Jimmy the Greek, who turned for the moment from his usual bailiwick of sports to politics, quoted Nixon a 100 to 1 favorite, and Galifianakis a 2-1 favorite. Whether the Greek was blinded by a common heritage or simply had ignored recent developments, the prediction on the Helms-Galifianakis race did not reflect what recent polls were suggesting. Jimmy the Greek, though, was right about Nixon. The president received 70% of the vote in the state, capturing many of the primary votes that had been cast for George

Wallace.

The president's coattails were long enough to bring North Carolina its first Republican senator and first Republican governor in the twentieth century. Nick Galifianakis lost his Senate race 54% to 46%, or somewhat over 120,000 votes. Helms had carried 60% of the upper-class white vote and majorities of all other white votes; on the other hand, Nick had almost 90% of the black vote. Nixon's popularity had certainly aided Helms, but the former television commentator, by bringing together social and economic traditionalists to the state Republican Party, not only contributed greatly to the rise of the party in the state but also "strengthened, indirectly but significantly, a traditionalist political agenda at local and state levels."

Elsewhere, Democrats, despite losses in North Carolina, New Mexico, Oklahoma and Virginia, saw their Senate majority increase by two seats from 55 to 57. The four losses were overcome by victories in Colorado, Iowa, Kentucky, South Dakota, Delaware, and Maine. Of special interest was the Delaware election, in which the incumbent Republican J. Caleb Boggs was unexpectedly defeated by the 29-year old Democrat Joseph R. Biden, Jr. Biden would turn 30, the minimum age for a Senator, later in the month. That youth had been a factor in the election cycle was confirmed in Maine by the ouster of 74-year-old Republican Senator Margaret Chase Smith by a 48-year old Democrat. Nick's defeat of Jordan in the Democratic primary was certainly in part a result of the age difference; however, with regard to Helms, who was 51, the seven-year difference was not a factor.

Nick's first electoral defeat was a distressing personal loss and a costly lesson that his style of personal, hands-on campaigning could not survive a well-financed, attacking media blitz. Substantially outspent, Galifianakis ended up with a $50,000 campaign debt. Russell Walker said "It took all of us a long time to get over that loss to Jesse. It was a real blow." Former Governor Sanford added that, although Nick continued to joke about the loss, it was really quite traumatic. In the final analysis Galifianakis had believed he could overcome the importance of money in a statewide campaign. Personally, he found it difficult to ask people for money. His energy was immense, but the days were not long enough for him to touch every voter's hand. His loss clouded his political future in the state. The Democratic establishment, which had never fully embraced this Greek-American, now blamed him for losing the Senate seat. Had Jordan won the Democratic primary, the politicos said, he would easily have defeated Helms.

In victory, Helms paid tribute to the "hundreds of young men and women" from the conservative Young Americans for Freedom, whose campaigning he credited with responsibility for the victory. At the same time, he denied that the appearance of President Richard Nixon in North Carolina on the Saturday before the election made much of a difference. Some observers, however, saw Nixon's presence, along with the president's claim that he needed Jesse in Washington, as a decisive factor. However, Helms said, he was most pleased "to have a part in demonstrating that the 'lib'rul' editors are virtually without influence –if those of us on the other side simply fight hard enough." Helms had long attacked newspaper editorialists; the fact that the large city dailies in North Carolina had backed his opponent now only confirmed the former broadcaster's opinion that they habitually supported the wrong policies and people.

Helms' strong, conservative views and the tenacity

with which he held them had always resonated in eastern North Carolina. Here, Republicans had made little headway before Helms, but these North Carolinians saw the same specter he did—one of an ever encroaching federal government, the erosion of family values, and the liberal belief in the ability of government to solve problems. Helms felt no discomfort when others called him a right-wing extremist. Not only did he bring new life to the Republican Party in the state, but he also spawned a national conservative movement. Helms had little in common with the party of Lincoln and Eisenhower and proudly declared "I'm not a Nixon Republican. I'm nobody's Republican or anything else." Yet it was the Republican Party that he helped refashion into one dedicated both to social and economic conservatism.

First appraised in Washington as "a right wing" crank whose tenure would be brief, he surprised his critics not only by winning reelection four times but also by filling the gap between Barry Goldwater's defeat in the presidential election of 1964 and Ronald Reagan's victory in 1980. Helms became known as "Senator No," as he and his supporters bottled up initiatives and forced Senate votes on positions that could not succeed, but which resulted in placing colleagues in embarrassing or vulnerable positions. For thirty years, he was the most visible representative of a state that had long viewed itself as moderate and balanced. Helms was neither. In five general elections, he never won by more than 55% of the votes. North Carolinians in that losing percentage were forced to explain how a so-called progressive Southern state was represented by a senator who eschewed moderation in any form. His character may be most vividly illustrated by the fact that while George Wallace and Strom Thurmond, two ardent segregationists, apologized for their resistance to the civil rights movement, Helms never did.

His death in July 2008 brought conflicting sentiments about his legacy. No matter which side one took, however, one tribute was consistent: that he always found time for North Carolinians who found their way to his office, and he responded to their needs with an efficiency that his strongest critics could not deny. When a person was frustrated by a problem with an agency of the federal government, they were advised to contact Helms' office. Seemingly, without fail, matters that had not been resolved for months would be quickly resolved. Even if people disagreed with his policies, they had to admire his commitment to be of effective service to his constituents in North Carolina, whether they voted for him or not.

What Helms introduced into modern-day political campaigning was the branding of an opponent as an "other," or "not one of us." Certainly Helms smeared Galifianakis with the liberal label, but what was most effective was the senator's success in fixing the image of the Greek-American as not being one of us, an outsider who was either to be feared, as others have been through the ages, or rejected. That ability to characterize Nick, who so long had been able to characterize himself as a true representative of North Carolina's interests (with a name that he even made fun of) as an outsider, threw the congressman off stride and forced him into a defensive posture. From the outset, Nick had been a political longshot and he regularly had to defend his record, but to have an opponent's characterization of him displace his own was the fatal blow. The fact that a majority of the state's voters concluded that Nick, a native North Carolinian, was not one of them was devastating. Nick had always assumed that "us" included him.

The key to successful negative campaigning lies in characterizing your opponent before you can be characterized.

In the Galifianakis-Helms race the Republican challenger defined Nick and forced him into a defensive posture. No amount of denials that this characterization was false or misleading could alter the image that had been planted in the public mind. There, the focus of the race was placed. The fact that Helms was certainly no supporter of President Nixon and that as a broadcaster he had expressed extreme views that were not shared by moderate North Carolinians was buried beneath the media barrage of the campaign's last month. None of the political advertising stressed Helms' qualifications. The most positive the campaign got in its blitz was the misleading claim that Nixon needed Helms. Those who knew Nick could not be taken in by the negative campaign, but, for those who did not, that type of campaign proved successful. It was less a matter of the quantity of ads than it was of which man succeeded in controlling the characterization of his opponent. Even if Nick had grasped the significance of this fact, it was contrary to both his nature and style of campaigning, which was to put forward one's own qualifications and implicitly indicate their superiority.

Galifianakis attributed his defeat to his being greatly outspent by Helms, but it was not only the disparity in campaign funds but also how those funds were used that explained the outcome. The effectiveness of Helms' use of money to buy time on the airwaves in that last month in order to stress a negative characterization of his opponent, was borne out by the fact that a 12% Galifianakis lead had become by election time an 8% deficit.

Nick had been caught up in the maelstrom of political change that doomed the politics of personal contact in favor of high cost media imaging. Many political commentators said that Galifianakis had mastered the art of politics, but it was an old style of politics that was dying out. This new style would send the cost of successful campaigning skyrocketing.

Galifianakis would have been a much different senator. Whether he could have survived in the Senate as long as Jesse Helms did is doubtful. Nick would have found, as he usually had, challengers within his own party. Also, with both a regional and national Republican resurgence, he would have had a tough battle in each general election. Money had always been a factor in elections, but now it seemed to be having a growing influence. Nick disliked and underemphasized fundraising, but successful candidates in the future would have to be fully committed to raising money in ways that made Nick uncomfortable. Perhaps his best political arena was a congressional district where he could personally meet the electorate and where everyone knew his name.

INTERLUDE 13

"He's Not One of Us:" Lessons and Legacy

The Galifianakis-Helms race has had lasting significance and the lessons it taught have become part the political landscape. They are as follows:

1) Negative campaigning works, and the sooner it is employed, the better.

2) Positions on issues and experience are of lessening importance, thereby leaving room for outliers who gain traction by proudly proclaiming that they are not politicians.

3) Money has become increasingly important because of the expense of media, especially television, advertising in fixing the image of one's opponent.

4) The old politics of personal contact has given way to a new politics of image shaping through the media.

5) Finally, although truth and facts have always been casualties of political campaigning, the wounds now suffered seem more serious.

Helms' success in etching his portrayal of Galifianakis into the public mind became a model that escaped the confines of the state's borders to become a significant element in subsequent campaigns throughout the nation. Just consider two recent presidential contests: George W. Bush versus John Kerry and John McCain versus Barack Obama. In the 2004 race the Bush campaign was able to fix the image of an indecisive man into the public mind resulting in the election of Bush to a second term. In the 2008 race a conflicted McCain resisted the advice to portray his opponent as an "other," until his slippage in the polls led McCain in a desperate move to try to do just that.

Then there is the campaign of Donald Trump, at the time of this writing the nominee of the Republican Party for president in 2016. Trump defines himself as a blunt, truth-talking businessman who could take his successful experience and apply it to the task of running the country as its president. Just like Helms, Trump denies that he is a politician, and therefore can "tell it like it is." Politicians, he says, do not have business experience, and more importantly have to dissemble. Furthermore, they have to be politically correct so as not to alienate potential supporters. Before his opponents could point to his immense wealth as a disability, Trump embraced his wealth and declared that he could finance his own campaign and not be beholden to rich donors.

When one or more of Trump's opponents or members of the press sought to put the candidate on the defensive, he refused to be put there. When asked whether he would apologize for his crude attacks on others, Trump simply said he would not. Would not his blunt words and attacks lessen his support in the polls? To the dismay of the political pundits, the answer was no. Could not members of the press simply replace the candidate's characterization of himself with their own? Again the answer was no. Instead, the press was forced to deal with Trump on his own terms. Trump had set the press' agenda. The candidate made his lack of political experience, which could have been a detriment to his candidacy, an asset and essentially removed it from further inspection. His critics were left with contending that successful business experience does not translate into useful training for the presidency, and that truth-telling does not require one to insult others. Politicians are dissembling wimps, said Trump, in contrast to himself, the forceful, plain-speaking, fearless leader who could be counted on to get things done.

In addition to the way negative campaigning has become a staple of the American political process, so also, has the identification of the Republican Party with conservatism. All the 2016 Republican presidential candidates, except for Trump, sought to don the authentic conservative mantle. One candidate, Senator Ted Cruz, went further yet in the direction of Helms, fostering the notion that conservatism can change the direction of the country only if conservatives refuse to compromise and work hard and consistently toward the goals of their political philosophy.

One final carryover from the Helms-Galifianakis race of 1972 is the relative success of attacking the media as a political tactic. Generally, these media attacks resonate well with the public. But then the bearer of bad or unflattering news has always been vulnerable.

CHAPTER XIV

Ending of a Political Career, 1973-1979

When one campaigns as Nick did, the personal stakes are quite high and it is hard to avoid interpreting electoral defeat as personal rejection. He could not understand how the double- digit lead he had in the polls in early October had disappeared. For over a year, Nick refused to talk publicly about his electoral loss. When he did, he attributed it first to the unpopularity of the Democratic candidate for President, George McGovern, that gave the incumbent Nixon especially long coattails, and second to the lack of support from other Democratic candidates. Nick hoped the defeat could be a wake-up call and suggested that the state Democratic Party raise resources that it would then distribute among the party's campaigners.

Nick was unprepared for his loss in 1972, his first in thirteen elections, but he was not discouraged from continuing his political career. Many of Galifianakis' supporters agreed with him and looked at the 1972 election result as only a momentary setback. Maybe Nick would not have to wait until 1978 when Helms would have to stand for reelection. Senator Sam Ervin's term ended in 1974. Even Nick would not seek to contest the party's nomination of Senator Sam, but perhaps the incumbent would decide to retire. As chairman of the Senate Committee investigating the Watergate break-in and the involvement of the White House in the affair, he was basking in the national spotlight. A decision to retire at this high point in his senatorial service was not out of the question. After all, at 77, he was older than Jordan was in 1972.

Relishing again the role of the underdog, Nick had to realize that retirement at the end of a term would bring into the race establishment candidates who would never have challenged an incumbent. Furthermore, Nick was blamed for losing the senatorial seat in 1972 to the Republicans. The prevailing wisdom was that no Republican, including Jesse Helms, could have ousted Jordan. Unlike Frank Porter Graham, who was devastated by his loss in 1950 and left politics, Nick seemed oblivious to such criticism, feeling that he could still rally voters to his side.

Nick wound up his congressional duties, emptied his office, and said good-bye to his staff in December 1972. He rejoined the law firm of Upchurch, Galifianakis and McPherson in Durham. For a brief time, he had a law practice in Washington as well. The power and glamour of the nation's capital was hard to leave behind.

When Sam Ervin did decide to retire in 1974 after nineteen years of service, claiming he was too old to complete another six-year term, the race for a successor seemed wide open. State attorney general Robert B. Morgan, who had been eyeing the seat even with Ervin in it, quickly announced his candidacy. He immediately became the establishment candidate. As state attorney general, he had gained some reputation as a protector of consumer interests.

Rather than plunge ahead and enter the race, Nick hesitated. The situation was what he had hoped for, but the campaign structure he had put together in 1972 had disintegrated. He worried about raising enough money to be competitive in the race to succeed Ervin. Galifianakis had been advised to stay out of the race to promote party unity, but even those naysayers were not ready to conclude that "the smiling Greek is dead politically." Nick, himself, said "I'm still resurrectable."

Finally, on February 25, 1974, two hours before the filing deadline, Nick announced his candidacy, making a total of ten candidates seeking Ervin's former seat. However, from the outset, seven of the candidates were not taken seriously. In addition to Morgan, the only other potentially competitive candidate was Henry Hall Wilson, a former aide to Presidents John F. Kennedy and Lyndon B. Johnson, and a former president of the Chicago Board of Trade. He had entered the contest as a moderate to challenge the more conservative Morgan. Nick's late entry into the campaign made things difficult both for himself and Wilson. They would have to compete "for the same contributors and organizational support." Nick still had a campaign debt of $50,000 left over from his race against Helms, and he faced some difficulty in revitalizing his former supporters. Also, the late entry put Galifianakis considerably behind Morgan, who had been quietly running even before Ervin had made his retirement official.

Election observers looked at the race as less issue-centered than character-centered. Voters were looking for sincerity, and Nick in responding to an inquiry said that he, also, believed that character was "the crucial issue." He said you need to demonstrate that "you can handle the job and that you do care." Certainly Galifianakis, of the three candidates, was the most vigorous, outgoing, and experienced, a combination of characteristics that had stood him well in his past political races.

Columnists Rowland Evans and Robert Novak saw Morgan as "a throwback to shrewd courthouse Democratic politicians of the old one-party South—canny, non-ideological and supremely flexible." His management of segregationist I. Beverly Lake's campaign against Terry Sanford in the gubernatorial race of 1960 and his support of the Speaker-Ban Law might lose him some votes, they wrote, but those positions helped ensure that he would not suffer from having the liberal label pinned on him. While Nick supported the impeachment of President Nixon, Morgan ducked the issue, having earlier praised Nixon for his actions and being unsure of just how strong Nixon sentiment was in the state. Morgan also supported the Vietnam war effort, and, in fact, refused to endorse Galifianakis' Senate bid in 1972 because of their differing views on the matter.

Nick's late entry into the race not only left him with little room to make up ground but it also denied him some of the newspaper coverage that had been such an important part of his earlier electoral successes. The newspapers were now filled with news about Nixon's imperiled future and the downfall of his associates. Morgan was the candidate backed by the establishment, and although Nick had defeated establishment candidates before, his campaign lacked the confidence and attention-grabbing activities that had attracted reporters and helped bring his earlier victories. Since 1972, the cost of running for office statewide had increased, bolstered by the rising cost of television ads. Wilson challenged his rival candidates to do what he had done—explain clearly in a campaign publication his positions on a number of issues. He pointed out that he had only spent $11,000 on television spots, while Nick had spent $40,000 and Morgan $124,000.

Tabulating expenditures on the eve of the primary, Nick reported $96, 908, Wilson $347, 956, and Morgan $399, 214. Charles B. Winberry, Morgan's campaign manager, criticized Wilson and Galifianakis for running their campaigns with money that came from out-of-state contributors. While Morgan got only 1.4% of his campaign contributions from non-North Carolinians, Wilson got 73.9% and Galifianakis 60.9%. How much this charge resonated with North Carolina voters is difficult to determine. When Pat Taylor, the early frontrunner for the Democratic nomination for governor in 1972, not only indicated his support for Nick but also sent a letter of endorsement to newspapers and to one thousand supporters in the state, Galifianakis was elated.

On the same day that Taylor's support of Nick was made public, newspapers carried a story saying that an ethics charge filed against Morgan with the North Carolina Bar had been dismissed. Earlier rumors had indicated that the North Carolina Bar would reprimand Morgan for his action as attorney general in filing a suit against five gas stations. When Nick suggested the possibility of a cover-up, Morgan was incensed, saying the accusation "may well be the dirtiest attack ever made on a political candidate in the history of the state." Despite the hyperbole of Morgan's response, Nick's ill-advised adoption of the rumor may only have backfired; certainly it revealed desperation in his campaign.

Morgan was annoyed about repeatedly being asked about two matters. The first was the possible impeachment of President Nixon. Since Nixon had won the state rather handily in 1972, Morgan was hesitant to alienate potential supporters by taking a position on Nixon. He tried to stop the questioning by saying that as a senator he might have to sit in judgment of the president and did not want to take a position now without being privy to all the relevant facts. The other issue that reporters did not ignore was Morgan's close identification with I. Beverly Lake. Did Morgan share the segregationist's views? Morgan, who felt he needed to court the black vote, tried to escape from Lake's orbit by saying that his role in Lake's campaigns was the result of a friendship he developed as a student at the Wake Forest University law school where Lake had taught.

For some reason, this explanation seemed to assure even black voters. How else can one understand why Morgan won the endorsement of the Durham Committee on the Affairs of Black People, a group that had long supported Nick's electoral efforts? Furthermore, Wilson's criticism of Morgan's embrace of consumer protection as "mere shadowboxing," and Galifianakis' insistence that it was illegal for Morgan to retain his office as attorney-general while campaigning for the Senate seat seemed to have no appreciable effect on voters.

Morgan was leading, but polls indicated that a quarter to a third of the voters were undecided on the eve of the primary. Nick had taken the most forceful stand on impeaching the president and put both his energy and gregarious nature behind his campaign effort. He urged a tax cut, and accused oil companies of manufacturing an energy shortage. In a three-person race, it seemed unlikely that a second primary could be avoided.

Ferrel Guillory, a political reporter for the *News & Observer*, questioned whether Nick, despite his vigorous campaigning, could overcome the challenges of a late start, fundraising difficulties, and the reassembling an organization that had been disbanded after his 1972 loss. He wrote: "Whether this type of personal campaigning can prevail in so short a time before an election in a state as large as North Carolina is the test confronting Galifianakis."

Nick would fail the test. To add to the humiliation, Morgan won the primary by 294,986 votes to Nick's 189, 815 votes, giving him just over 50% to Nick's 32%, thus eliminating the possibility of a second primary. Despite spending a good deal of money, Wilson only received 67, 242 votes. Morgan went on to overwhelm the Republican candidate, William E. Stevens, who easily won the Republican nomination over two other candidates in the May primary. The state attorney general garnered almost 63% of the vote in the general election.

Morgan had been replaced as attorney general by a Republican appointee, and *The Messenger*, a weekly paper in Rockingham County, suggested that the Democratic Executive Committee, despite a bevy of challengers, should draft Nick Galifianakis to run for the post. Its argument was that Nick would be a unifier for a party that seemed in disarray. The paper cited Nick's commitment to party unity by noting that, after his recent loss, he had written to his supporters urging them to support Morgan. Referring to Nick's loss to Helms, the editorial added: "No man better knows the bitter taste of a defeat caused by the failure of the party to close ranks and offer a united front in the general election."

Terry Sanford concluded that the recent attempt to gain a Senate seat was an attempt on Nick's part to "vindicate his earlier loss." The former governor and presidential candidate said that "the cards had already been dealt" and that Nick had gotten into a situation that he "couldn't win." Sanford was right when he said that Nick felt that his very existence was justified by his holding political office. Nick's name came up as a possible candidate for federal district judge in 1977, but Galifianakis still had his eye on a rematch with Helms. That rematch, however, would never occur.

Nick had been badly wounded by his defeat by Morgan

in 1974, but he and his supporters still did not believe that the wound would prove to be politically fatal. Confident of his ability, Galifianakis believed that he could continue to sell his credentials and character to a majority of the state's voters. He was an honest, thoughtful and hard-working politician who truly believed that he represented the people of the state well and responsibly. What more could voters ask? Because of this emphasis on his honesty and character, the next blow he received would deepen the wound and bury him politically.

He was to become immersed in a political scandal that some observers initially believed could dwarf Watergate, which indeed had forced Richard Nixon to resign the presidency. What gave Koreagate, as it was called, such potential was its breadth, the sheer number of congressmen and senators involved, and the suspicion that members of Congress could be bribed to enact the agenda of a foreign country. The country was South Korea, which had come into existence under United Nations auspices when the northern half of the peninsula refused to participate in national elections in 1950. A war fought primarily by Americans to prevent the unification of the peninsula under the aegis of the Communist North had been brought to an end in July, 1953 with the division of the country into two parts. A substantial contingent of American forces would remain in the country.

By the mid-1970s American forces in South Korea had been reduced from 60,000 to a little over 35,000. Apparently the South Korean government decided it needed more support from the U.S. Congress on this and other matters and appropriated at least $500,000 to secure such support. In late December 1976 Justice Department investigators reported that they had accumulated enough evidence to consider the possibility of criminal prosecution of certain individuals. On the horizon were investigations by three House committees and one in the Senate, along with others in various departments of the government.

One of the important missing witnesses was a Korean businessman and socialite, known as Tongsun Park, who threw lavish Washington parties. He was suspected of being an agent of the South Korean government. The *Washington Post* reported that Park had secured congressional help in buying commodities, in stifling criticism of South Korea's president, in maintaining and even increasing American troop levels in the country, in gaining tariff relief for imported goods from his country, in obtaining contracts paid for with American aid, and in advancing his own business activities. In the *Post's* April 27, 1977 article, under the headline "13 Congressmen Aided Tongsun Park," Nick Galifianakis was named with eleven other former members of Congress and one sitting member. By July, the number had been increased to 115, almost 20% of the total membership of the House and Senate.

A number of congressmen and former congressmen readily admitted that they had received cash campaign contributions from Park but insisted that they had always assumed that he was a foreign businessman, not an agent of a foreign government. Until 1974, there was no ban on American legislators receiving contributions from foreign businessmen, only from agents of a foreign government. Prosecutors would have to prove that the legislator had been bribed to take a particular course of action in his legislative role. What made this task even more difficult was the protection the United States Constitution offered: "The Senators and Representatives . . . shall in all Cases, except Treason, Felony and Breach of the Peace, be privileged from Arrest [while in or going to or from Congress] . . . and for any Speech or Debate in either House, they shall not be questioned in any other Place." The provision shifted prosecutorial attention to former congressmen.

Park had never registered as a foreign agent, nor did the South Korean government so acknowledge him. As relations between the two countries deteriorated, South Korea refused President Jimmy Carter's request that Park answer an indictment. Leon Jaworski, special prosecutor in the Watergate affair, had been persuaded to take charge of the investigation of the House Ethics Committee into the matter. Park was granted immunity from prosecution by the Justice Department for his testimony, but the agreement did not require him to appear before the House Ethics Committee.

When Nick's name came up in the *Post* story as one who aided Park, the former congressman acknowledged that he knew Park socially, but denied that he aided Park in any way. He did say that his office may have sent Park letters thanking him for invitations to parties. Galifianakis also said that he had not been contacted by the Justice Department. Nick did concede that he may have received a check from Park for $500 as a contribution to one of his campaigns, but that his policy was to return contributions from foreign nationals. Four of the congressmen mentioned in the *Post* story, including Nick, had served on the House Appropriations Committee, a body that oversaw much foreign spending.

Eventually matters were worked out and Park agreed to testify before the House Ethics Committee. Although he denied being a foreign agent, he did provide the committee with detailed information on his disbursement of $850,000. Most of the money went to three former members of Congress who helped him become South Korea's exclusive rice dealer. Those three men were Representatives Otto E. Passman of Louisiana, Richard C. Hanna of California, and Cornelius E. Gallagher of New Jersey. They all received over $200,000. As the exclusive rice dealer, Park earned a $9,000,000 commission on purchases through the United States Food for Peace program.

Park said that the total amount given to Nick Galifianakis was $10,500. Nick had always acknowledged the $500; he had returned a check in that amount, although Park had provided Nick with a $500 credit at the exclusive Georgetown Club instead. What was new was the mention of a $10,000 donation to Galifianakis' Senate campaign in 1972. There was nothing illegal about a $10,000 contribution in 1972, because it happened before a $1000 limit had been imposed in the wake of Watergate. The failure to report a campaign contribution was illegal in 1972, but the offense carried a three-year statute of limitations. Moreover, if it were not listed as a campaign contribution, it would be treated as an addition to Nick's income, thus leaving open the possibility of action by the Internal Revenue Service.

The *News & Observer*, which had been a supporter of Nick in his senatorial campaign in 1972, now noted that Galifianakis' "previously clean record in state and national politics has come under a dark cloud." The newspaper found Nick's assurance that he never did any favors for Park an unsatisfactory response for a person whose "ethical conduct and personal probity" is at stake. Galifianakis, the editorial concluded, "owes a full and frank statement to all North Carolinians." His hometown morning paper, the *Durham Morning Herald*, agreed, saying that if their favorite son was guilty of no wrongdoing "the people of this district deserve to know it, especially those who gave him their time, money and, in no small measure, their hearts because they thought he stood for the things they believed in, including decency in politics." Even his campaign manager, Russell Walker, shared the paper's sentiments, saying "I'm greatly surprised at this. I really believed in him. I've had a lot of calls from people who worked for us in that campaign. A lot of them are greatly upset."

Before Nick responded, his campaign treasurer in 1972 and present law partner, Roger Upchurch, said that Park was never listed as a contributor of any amount on the record of campaign finances. When Galifianakis did respond, he again asserted that Park "never asked me to do anything for him and I have done nothing for him." He then added that he would not comment on specifics until Park had finished testifying. Park gave further details about the contribution. The Korean said Nick had asked for the contribution and had sent an aide to Park's house to pick up the cash. Furthermore, Park recalled that Galifianakis later thanked him for the contribution. The House Committee, before which Park was testifying, indicated that it would call another person to corroborate Park's recollection. That person was Barbara Fletcher, Nick's longtime staffer, who had served as an unofficial campaign treasurer and now worked for Ike Andrews, Galifianakis' successor as 4th District congressman. Fletcher said she had been instructed, by whom she could not recall, to fly to Washington in very early November 1972 and pick up the cash at Park's home. The Korean businessman gave her an envelope stuffed with $100 bills and said "Give this to my friend Nick." Apparently she took the money to her home and placed it in a dresser drawer without reporting its receipt, dispensing the cash as it was needed in the last five days of the campaign. She said she used it for meals for campaign volunteers, refreshments for hospitality functions, and maybe to pay poll workers. What was left, she said she gave to Nick. Then she added that Galifianakis had said "something like 'Only you and Mr. Park directly participated in that transaction and so only you two can testify to it'." She also testified that she and Nick had discussed the transaction in later years. As recently as last June 25, 1977, she said Nick told her that when the FBI asked him if he had received a $15,000 contribution from Park he, in good conscience, said no and offered no further explanation.

The long, drawn out Koreagate investigation achieved its first success in March 1978 when former Democratic congressman Richard T. Hanna from California pleaded guilty to receiving over $200,000 to assist Park in his business dealings. The indictment had forty counts. In return for the guilty plea to conspiring to defraud the government, thirty-nine other charges were dropped. Another former member of Congress, Otto Passman was also indicted for taking payments of a similar amount from Park and for a failure to pay income tax on the money. However, he was acquitted by a jury in his home state of Louisiana. The indictment against Park was dismissed, though the Internal Revenue Service claimed that he owed $5 million in back taxes. Although the Korean had named many sitting members of Congress as recipients of his largess, only Hanna had confessed guilt. The former congressman served less than a year in prison.

On June 16, 1978, Nick found himself named in a Doonesbury cartoon appearing in many newspapers. Gary Trudeau, the cartoonist, had a storyline that called attention to Koreagate and in one strip had incorporated a coupon addressed to House Speaker Thomas (Tip) O'Neill recommending hearings be held on the scandal. In that coupon Nick's name was listed, with three others, for checking by the sender asking for more information about the persons listed.

Nick had nothing to fear from the House Ethics Committee, for it had no jurisdiction over former members. However, Millicent Fenwick, a member from New Jersey, did suggest that the discrepancies between Nick's testimony before the committee in closed session and Park's and Fletcher's testimony be referred by the panel to the Justice Department for the bringing of perjury charges.

A scandal at its outset that some predicted would overshadow Watergate had fizzled out with a single criminal conviction of a former congressman under a guilty plea. Perhaps this failure to achieve much led the Justice Department to pick up on Fenwick's suggestion in April 1979 and to indict Nick Galifianakis based upon his alleged perjury before the House Ethics Committee.

Galifianakis said his lawyer, Barry Levine, a local criminal attorney, had advised him not to say anything about the charges, but Nick did release a statement saying, "I am deeply disturbed by the events which have transpired today in Washington. I regret any pain or embarrassment which this may cause my family, friends, supporters and colleagues. I hope all of you know that I treasure my years of public service to my state and to my country." The criminal charge was based on Nick's denial in his testimony before the committee that he had received the $10,000 contribution from Park. If convicted, Galifianakis faced a sentence of up to five years in jail and a $2,000 fine. On April 17, 1979 he entered a plea of not guilty. Levine suggested that Nick was being used as a scapegoat to help justify the enormous expenses of the Koreagate investigation. The lawyer noted that no sitting member of Congress had been indicted.

Clearly, Nick had not acknowledged the contribution. Still, the fact that an investigation that promised so much and produced so little had led to his being pursued for this transgression seemed less than fair and equitable to him. As he assessed his situation, Galifianakis, despite hiring Levine, used his own expertise to guide his defense. Both as a congressman and as a lawyer, Nick was always well-versed in procedural matters; he understood that before substantive matters were addressed a claim had to meet procedural requirements. In addition, if he was not able to get the indictment squashed on procedural grounds, he would have to endure a trial in which a disinterested party, his former aide Barbara Fletcher, backed up Park's testimony.

Nick's hand can clearly be seen behind the motion presented by Levine in June to District Judge Charles Richey in Washington, D. C. The motion listed several reasons why the indictment should be dismissed: the fact that the committee failed to get House approval to refer the matter to the Justice Department; the fact that the questioning took place before a single committee member without the approval of a majority of the committee; the fact that Galifianakis was never apprised of the nature of the committee's inquiry; the fact that a single committee member did not constitute "a competent tribunal;" the fact that a single member was not authorized to administer the oath to him; and finally the fact that the grand jury process was abused when the Justice Department relied upon an affidavit from Park even though he was in Washington and available to testify in person. Judge Richey got no further than the first matter, the lack of a full House referral of the matter to the Justice Department, saying that this failure to follow House rules seemed to him to make any case against Galifianakis "fatally flawed." The Justice Department attorney, John

Kotelly, asked the judge to issue a subpoena for pertinent House records, but the judge refused. Instead Kotelly was given two weeks in which to convince Judge Richey not to dismiss the indictment.

Kotelly responded by claiming that the rules cited in the motion to dismiss did not apply to a former member of Congress. Furthermore, he argued that Galifianakis lost his ability to protest when he did not resist providing testimony before the single committee member whom he now contended was not authorized to administer an oath and take his testimony. Judge Richey found the position of the Justice Department unconvincing and dismissed the case. The Justice Department threatened to appeal the ruling, but eventually the Solicitor General decided that there was no merit in the Department's position, thus freeing Nick from any charges stemming from the Park contribution. Levine said "a long and tortuous ordeal" had now been brought to an end. When a 36-count indictment against Park was dismissed on August 16, 1979, the tempest in a teapot called Koreagate was finally brought to an end.

When Nick got word that the dismissal would not be appealed, he expressed relief and thankfulness for the support of family and friends. He then added: "This experience was an unpleasant one and one that threatened to cloud everything I worked for while I was in public office and destroy everything which I have tried to stand for throughout my life—so, while it has been a painful experience, I am trying to learn and grow from it, and I plan in the coming months to utilize in a constructive way the insights and knowledge that have been realized from this entire experience."

During the ordeal Jesse Helms had been reelected; any chance of a rematch had been dashed by Koreagate. If the scandal had little effect elsewhere, it certainly contributed to bringing the political career of Nick Galifianakis to an end. Friends and associates would try to nudge him into running for political office, and each election season would rekindle the urge, but even ever-optimistic Nick recognized that his career in politics was over. Even without Koreagate, as the 1974 race against Morgan confirmed, Nick had no support from the state's Democratic Party. The party establishment had never fully embraced Galifianakis, and his loss of a Senate seat would never be forgiven. Of course, the party leaders had little interest in examining their own role in the loss or acknowledging the larger forces that shaped the 1972 election.

John E. Semonche

FINALE

Life After Politics

Nick would make a brief return to Washington soon after his initial departure in 1972, setting up an office for a New York lawyer who wanted a presence in the nation's capital. Galifianakis was encouraged by a Washington power broker named Jim Brown and a friend in the media, Jack Williams, to do just that. Nick accepted, and in a short tenure served many clients, including Colonel Saunders of fried chicken fame and Zsa Zsa Gabor, the actress. The tenure was short because legal difficulties of the New York lawyer convinced Nick that the relationship should be terminated.

Although over the years Nick would visit Washington for social and political occasions like inaugurations and meetings of former congressmen, one particular project kept him travelling to the nation's capital. In 1991, one of his former campaign workers, an immigration lawyer named Jack Pinnix needed assistance. The matter involved a Chinese immigrant, Charlie Tsui, also known as Charlie Two Shoes. While in China after the end of World War II, several Marines, part of Love Company, had befriended a boy who lived in a mud hut just beyond the compound. They gave him food and clothing, taught him English, and sent him to school and church. When the Communists took control in 1949, the Marines were forced to leave. Charlie's connection with the American troops led the government to make him a political prisoner. When Charlie was eventually freed, he got in touch with the Marines who then worked to bring him to the United States, an effort that finally proved successful in 1983. Two years later Charlie's family followed him. The family eventually opened up a restaurant in Chapel Hill. Charlie had been granted residency by the Nixon administration and could indeed work in the United States, but INS regulations precluded the granting of a green card, part of the required path to the citizenship that Charlie and his family desired.

At this point, Jack Pinnix sought Galifianakis' help. Nick concluded that the best approach was to get Congress to pass a private bill authorizing green card status and permanent residency to Charlie and his family. One problem was that the use of such private bills had declined because of abuse and now could only succeed if no one in either house of Congress objected. A single 'No' vote would doom the bill. Nick decided that the Senate would be the best place to start, for if the Senate acceded, he felt, so would the House. Galifianakis then convinced North Carolina's Terry Sanford, now serving in the Senate, to introduce the bill. Senator Sanford joined the many supporters of Charlie, including former President Ronald Reagan and the Commandant of the Marine Corps, General Al Gray. The bill received the unanimous consent required. In the House it was referred to the Judiciary Committee, headed by Romano Mazzoli, who did not like private bills. Nick prevailed upon their friendship to get Mazzoli to yield, but proceedings were then held up by an objection raised by a House member based on the rumor that Charlie was not a political prisoner but rather had been imprisoned for stealing silk.

By the time the State Department had cleared Charlie, Congress had adjourned, and the process had to be restarted. In the meantime, Sanford had been defeated, and the bill was now introduced by Congressman David Price, who represented Chapel Hill. Letters from the Marines and many others, whose attention had been drawn to the case by articles in *Parade* magazine and *Reader's Digest*, poured into Congress. However, Price's bill never came to a vote because Pinnix and Galifianakis believed, correctly, that a broader law passed in the wake of the Tiananmen Square protest granting asylum to Chinese dissidents covered all Chinese in the United States without green cards, including Charlie and his family. Charlie initially objected to his being grouped with dissidents who had fled China, but he finally realized that this might be the only way to reach his goal of American citizenship. The private bill approach could only be employed when no other avenue to success was available. Taking advantage of the dissident law, Charlie and his family became American citizens.

Back in Durham, Nick became what he had started out as—a general legal practitioner handling everything from criminal matters to estates. As other local lawyers narrowed their practices, Nick expanded his, taking on cases other lawyers refused because of their assessment of the case as a loser, because of their unfamiliarity with the relevant law, or because they saw no financial payoff. His wife, Lou, said that Nick and Don Quixote shared a determination "to fix the unfixable, no matter what others say." The difference, however, was that Nick often proved that what others deemed unfixable was indeed fixable

Galifianakis never worried much about his clients' ability to pay. If they needed legal help, he was there to provide it. In fac,t he did so much legal work pro bono that his legal secretary, when asked whether she had a nickname for Nick, she thought for a moment and came up with the incredibly apt "Probono Polysyllabus." No case was too complicated; no case exceeded his grasp. As other lawyers shied away from unfamiliar legal matters, Nick was ready to do the research required to have confidence in proceeding with the matter. His general practice was truly general, and what is more important, he never grew too old to find excitement in learning new things. As a neighbor remarked, he shared with the best of academics a love of learning that kept him young.

He found it difficult even as he reached his mid-80s to close his legal practice. How could he refuse his help to the people who he had served so long, clients who knew no other lawyer? As with his political career, he wanted to serve. And if the arena of service was now smaller than his potential had suggested, he made the most of it with good humor and the fervent belief that wrongs should be righted.

At 88 Nick Galifianakis is still stopped by people who remember his time in politics, some of whom can still sing his campaign song in its entirety.

ACKNOWLEDGEMENTS

First and foremost, I am indebted to my daughter, Laura S. Jones, who realized that, with the passing of my wife of almost 53 years, her father needed a project to fill the void. She encouraged me to dust off the draft of this book that I had written during my final years as a professor of history at the University of North Carolina at Chapel Hill and complete the research and writing that remained to be done. She convinced me that there was a good story to be told and shared with others.

Next to be recognized, of course, is the subject of the book, Nick Galifianakis, my good friend and next door neighbor for the last 46 years. His gait may have slowed, but his mind remains sharp and his memory is astonishing. Who, for instance, remembers the names of their first, second, and third grade teachers? Well, Nick does.

Thanks also to the unfailingly helpful librarians at the University of North Carolina, Duke University and the Durham Public Library's North Carolina Collection for their work in aiding my research effort.

Finally, I want to thank the good folks at Tidal Press for their support, editorial acumen, and commitment to the project.

John E. Semonche

A NOTE ON SOURCES AND FURTHER READING

The text relies substantially on the Papers of Nick Galifianakis. Although deteriorating, inadequately stored, and uncatalogued, they include a wealth of material mostly from his days in public office. The Papers include hand written notes, pictures, awards, articles, correspondence, legislative summaries, copies of the many speeches he made, among the other matter a public man, who discards little, accumulates. The Papers also include large notebooks of pasted-in newspaper articles, primarily covering his campaigns for federal office. These articles have been supplemented by others in newspapers, including those from outside the state of North Carolina. Nick's high school years are chronicled in issues of the Durham High School newspaper, the *Hi-Rocket*, which are also in the Papers.

Of almost equal importance to all the other sources has been the exceptional memory of Nick Galifianakis that the author has plumbed over a period of ten years or so. The stories stored in his memory could not always be verified by independent sources, but those that could give credibility to those that, because of the absence of relevant material, cannot.

For the material on Durham, the author has relied upon the following: W. C. Dula and A. C. Simpson, *Durham and Her People: Combining History and Who's Who in Durham of 1949 and 1950* (Durham: Citizens Press, 1951); and William Kenneth Boyd, *The Story of Durham: City of the New South* (Durham: Duke University Press, 1925).

Information on the Greek community in the city is drawn from a 25th Anniversary Album, published by St. Barbara's Greek Orthodox Church in 1970.

The Duke University material is drawn from William E. King, *If Gargoyles Could Talk: Sketches of Duke University* (Durham: Carolina Academic Press, 1997); and Robert F. Durden, *The Launching of Duke University 1924-1949* (Durham: Duke University Press, 1993).

For matters of North Carolina state government generally, see the *North Carolina Manual* for the appropriate years. The session laws are available online at www.ncleg. net for public laws from 1963 and local laws from 1959.

The material on the Speaker Ban Law is mostly drawn from William J. Billingsley, *Communists on Campus: Race, Politics, and the Public University in Sixties North Carolina* (Athens: University of Georgia Press, 1999).

For Nick's years in Congress (1967-1972), see the *Congressional Record*. Nick served in the 90[th,] 91st and 92nd Congresses. Those years' session laws can be found in *United States Statutes at Large,* vols. 79-84 or online for instance at www.gpo.gov/fdsys/pkg/STATUTE-79/ content-detail.html. For the membership of the various Congresses, see for instance http://history.house.gov/Congressional-Overview/Profiles/90th/.

Information on North Carolina and Southern Politics can be found in Numan V. Bartley and Hugh D. Graham, *Southern Politics and the Second Reconstruction* (Baltimore: Johns Hopkins University Press, 1975); Paul Luebke, *Tar Heel Politics 2000* (Chapel Hill: University of North Carolina Press, 1998); Rob Christensen, *The Paradox of Tar Heel Politics: The Personalities, Elections and Events*

That Shaped Modern North Carolina, 2ⁿᵈ ed., Revised and Updated (Chapel Hill: University of North Carolina Press, 2010); and Tom Eamon, The *Making of a Southern Democracy: North Carolina Politics From Kerr Scott to Pat McCrory* (Chapel Hill: University of North Carolina Press, 2014).

For material dealing with Jesse Helms and state and national politics, see William A. Link, *Righteous Warrior: Jesse Helms and the Rise of Modern Conservatism* (New York: St. Martin's Press, 2008); and Bryan Hardin Thrift, *Conservative Bias: H ow Jesse Helms Pioneered the Rise of Right-Wing Media and Realigned the Republican Party* (Gainesville: University Press of Florida, 2014)

The full story of Charlie Tsui is well told in Michael Peterson and Daniel Perlmutt, *Charlie Two Shoes and the Marines of Love Company* (Annapolis: Naval Institute Press, 1998).

For a comparison of Nick with his nephew, Zach Galifianakis and their respective campaigns (Nick's in the real world and Zach's in the world of Hollywood), see the author's piece on the editorial pages of the *Durham Herald-Sun* and Raleigh's *News & Observer* for April 18, 2012 and April 19, 2012 respectively.

Should any reader have need for a precise reference for a particular matter covered in the text, feel free to contact the author by email at semche@email.unc.edu. He may be able to provide it.

John E. Semonche

PHOTOGRAPHY CREDITS

287

All photographs and cartoons appearing in this book came from the personal archives of Nick Galifianakis and are used with his permission and authorization.

The photographers are unknown, except as noted below.

p. 44	Campus Photos
p. 68	Larry Martin of the Herald Sun
p. 82	Lt. L.M. Burdette
p. 107	John Sink (cartoon)
p. 113	A.P. wire
p. 168	Burton Berinsky
p. 175	Ron Snipes
p. 218	Dev O'Neill
p. 235	Charles Holland
p. 237	Harold Moore of the Herald Sun
p. 242	Bob Zschiesche of the Greensboro Daily News (cartoon)

John E. Semonche

CPSIA information can be obtained
at www.ICGtesting.com
Printed in the USA
LVOW11s1657300117
522613LV00006B/1045/P